SELF-EMPLOYED

and

PROFITABLE

LESSONS IN BUSINESS

SELF-EMPLOYED

and

PROFITABLE

Creating a profitable business and achieving financial
independence through self-employment

C.C. VANNCE

small BUSINESS
FINANCIAL

This edition has been cataloged by the Library of Congress as Self-Employed and Profitable.

2014 Sennav Solutions, LLC
P.O. Box 592001
San Antonio, TX 78259

First Edition: September 2014
ISBN: 978-0-9908399-0-3 (Paperback)

To all the self-employed people who work hard to build their businesses and create a bright future for their families; you are a pillar of strength, a force stimulating our economy, a gift to the many people who depend on your entrepreneurial spirit. May God bless your efforts, this book is for you!

"The purpose of every merchant is to make a lawful and reasonable profit so as to keep up his business."

~ LUCA PACIOLI

CONTENTS

WHAT TO EXPECT FROM THIS BOOK

In part one, **chapter one** sheds light on who is truly considered self-employed, and the general idea of what being self-employed is all about. It is also the starting point of your study about what being profitable means. As you move through **chapter two** you will begin to understand the mindset differences between that of an employee and a successfully self-employed person. You will learn how to make a smooth and successful transition from working at a job to running your business without the fear of failure. Chapter two also provides 120 low to no cost ideas for self-employment.

Part two, **chapter three** is where you will learn how the pieces are connected to make a business work. It's the introduction to the profit formula and covers in details how to put your ideas, dreams or vision into a plan. It covers how to determine how much you need to sell (retail or services) to make a profit, and business operating tools to assess your progress. We begin part three with **chapter four**, here you will be exposed to your choices of business structures and what the tax impact to each will be, this offers you insights that will help you make a well informed decision. **Chapter five** covers the business taxes that every self-employed person should know about, including quarterly estimates, and why you pay taxes. We wrap up part three with **chapter six** where you will learn about the necessities that will strengthen your business establishment, including bookkeeping, business insurance types, e-business, home office, commercial leases and much more.

Chapter seven is the beginning of part four. Here you will learn what impacts your ability to generate revenue and how to overcome common challenges that prevent many business owners from reaching their revenue potential. You will learn cost-effective marketing ideas, how to increase your revenue streams, and make a profit. **Chapter eight** digs deep into the three most relevant cost categories, what impacts cash the most and strategies to keep cost under control. Chapter eight also shows the ten warning signs that your business maybe failing and what to do to correct it. In **chapter nine** you will find out about how business owners build wealth, the potential obstacles and how to attain financial independence. The special treat in this chapter are the five time tested lessons for achieving financial independence. We wrap up in **chapter ten** with some of the challenges that business owners face on their journey to success and some solutions on how to overcome them. Throughout this book are examples, scenarios, and explanations to help you understand, so that you can operate your business with confidence. Business principles remain the same no matter which country you operate in around the world. However, beware that tax and other governing laws are different from country to country. This book takes into account the United States tax and governing laws.

INTRODUCTION

"The man who acquires the ability to take full possession of his own mind may take possession of anything else to which he is justly entitled."

~ ANDREW CARNEGIE

Your "aha!" moment, a sudden realization of what you need to do to move your life forward financially. A bold step towards a better future, not because you know exactly what to do but because you have chosen to put an end to what seems like an endless cycle of living paycheck to paycheck. After much pondering, sleepless nights, and prayers, you decided to dive right in and start your own business. Perhaps you have not made up your mind completely about it, but you know for sure that you do not want to continue in a cycle of financial despair. Sometimes it's like a battle going on in your mind as you try to stay hopeful about the future, but the ups and downs of the economy and the instability of the job market make you feel uncomfortable. The ongoing talks about the wealth inequality does not help the situation either, the rich getting richer and the middle class falling closer to the poverty line.

No matter the era, wealth and poverty seems to be a conversation that never goes away. However, the world has made an amazing transition from wealth only being inherited to wealth being self-made. Part of what causes the disparity between wealth and poverty is the lack of knowledge. What I am referring to is the lack of understanding about proper money management and how to use money to achieve financial independence. There's much information about how to work towards financial independence using salaries and wages even though some do not put it into practice. But many people who have decided to venture off into business for themselves do not understand how to operate and grow their business the right way. In an effort to find learning resources for my clients to study on how to grow their businesses as self-employed people, to my dismay there was not much out there and this is why I chose to write this book. As a tax and business consultant I started my professional career straight out of college as an auditor for Deloitte and eventually transitioned years later into being an independent tax and business consultant after I left KPMG.

I quickly found out that many business owners really do not understand what it takes to be profitable in business. Unfiled tax returns, back taxes, disorganized books, money mismanagement, commingling of personal and business funds, constantly busy but never accomplishing much, poor collections, bad payment behaviors, incorrect business structures, unnecessary debt and the list goes on. I did find one thing in common among these business owners, they wanted to do right, but they did not know how to do it. My desire to help them lead to many intimate conversations as they all expressed their hopes, fears and frustrations. But it wasn't all bad; many business owners are not totally lost, they just don't know how to connect all the pieces. After all many of them have done a great job doing the best they can with their businesses, but yet to maximize their potential. Various self-made successful business owners started small and put into practice good business principles and built their business gradually. The story of Sara Blakely is one to be admired, the founder of Spanx, Inc., a multi-million-dollar undergarment company that produces slimming bodywear and so much more for women and men. Sara, who used to sell fax machines door-to-door, started her company with only $5,000 and grew it to a billion dollar company; she did most of the work to build Spanx herself until her company was in a position to bring on staff. How Spanx came into existence has become an inspiration for many aspiring business owners around the world.

WHERE DID THINGS GO WRONG?

Many people who used business ownership as a path to financial freedom managed their money wisely, investing their profits in assets that produce income as well as those that appreciate in value. This notion is clearly highlighted in *Why "A" students work for "C" students*: "The rich have the financial education to acquire passive income. With financial education, the rich have the ability to increase income and reduce taxes by doing what the government wants done." The book also states that "They work hard to acquire assets, that put more money into their pockets and allow them to keep (thanks to better tax rates) more of what they earn." The financial disparity problem in my opinion is in part what people do with their earnings. Wealth is acquired over time, so during the good economic years the wealthy take their earnings from assets like business equity, securities, and real estate and reinvested them back into those assets to grow. Each of the assets mentioned are examples of investments that produce income which is explained further in this book. As a result, their wealth grows over time. When the economy takes a downward turn, their assets still performed well "overall" because of the income generated from these assets throughout the years. There will still be some losses, but in general they will have an increase in wealth because of the earnings generated in the good economic times, and their ability to safeguard their assets against inflation. For example, if the market value of real estate property goes down because foreclosures are on the rise, rents will usually go up because there will be a demand for places to rent—people still need somewhere to stay. For those who own rental real estate, their cash flow from the rental income will more than likely increase, while the fixed mortgage payments remain unchanged. Further, most real estate is held for the long term, so the decline to the market value of the property is temporary and will increase in the future when property values rise.

A down economy is usually an opportune time for real estate investors to buy more real estate at very low prices using income generated from other assets and low cost debt. These successful business owners continue to apply savvy business principles (like buy low, sell high) to grow their Net Worth and increase their streams of income. Unfortunately, while the financially educated get richer, so many others during an economic depression experience financial hardship because they did not manage their earnings wisely when the economy was good; and they are not financially educated enough to identify opportunities in a depressed economy—so they miss the opportunities available.

During the 2007-2008 economic downturn there was a significant decline in the value of stocks and real estate property; the people impacted by the recession the most where not sure what to do, reacted too late or were not able to identify the warning signs. Experience can be a very harsh teacher at times, but you learn from those experiences and rebuild with what's left. When you have a good financial education and an understanding of fundamental business principles you can always build again. In addition, being able to recognize good and bad opportunities when it is presented is also a key factor in building a solid financial picture. Opportunities do not always come we want them to, sometimes it shows up unexpectedly and we have to either seize the opportunity by faith or reject it by faith. In business, risk is always present, but you can reduce the level of risk by planning. You can also apply proven business principles; use your experiences and your instincts to help you navigate your way through the business process.

Perhaps you are like many of us who did not come from families that were educated in the art of wealth building, and over the years you've wondered why you were not making progress in your own finances; even with a business. You are aware that your financial state is not healthy and you want to know what to do. Well, now you can use the lessons in this book as a guide and reference source to help you change your financial condition. Information alone does not change your situation, but rather putting into practice the things you have learned is what will help you. When you have been exposed to financial education, it is your responsibility to use that information to change your condition, because you now have the knowledge and tools to do so. Sometimes, your answered prayer does not come in a tangible form, but in an intangible gift called knowledge and it is up to you what you do with it.

THE COURAGE TO DO, REBUILD, AND GO ON

Kudos to you for stepping out and charting your own course. Self- employment is certainly not for everyone, but if it is in you to try—you might as well do it the right way. This of course does not mean you will not encounter challenges, but you will have the knowledge and understanding to help you operate your business confidently. Self-employment is not the only way to financial independence, but for many people it is the most cost effective way to start—depending on your area of expertise. For example, consultants, architects, and e-business owners can start out working from a home office, which will allow them to save on lease cost.

Every self-employed person who puts forth the effort has the ability to take their business to the next level and use their earnings to build a healthier financial life. Although, as a self-employed person you are still physically doing the work, you will discover later in this book what to do in order to transition your business into one that does not depend upon you being there all the time. To achieve your goals, you must be willing to do the work. I often relate people who want to see a change in their business condition but never do anything about it, to a person who complains about wanting to lose weight and become healthier, but have never taken the time to exercise and eat right. Nothing changes until you make up your mind to act on it.

So, life gave you lemons and you've been making lemonade, but you believe there's got to be more that life has to offer—so you decided to open a lemonade stand. Perhaps you are just managing your business as best as possible—one day at a time, and you do realize that you don't have it all together—that you need help. I commend you for that; it takes self- awareness and guts to reach out for help.

Whatever happened up until this point does not matter anymore, put it behind you and move forward. We all make mistakes and nobody has it all together, you are not alone. It's a new day now, and time to structure your business for profitability. And I know that you are determined to make your business work; to learn the real secret to success that actually is not a secret at all. It's just unknown to many, primarily because of the shift to fast money making tactics. So the principles that people call secrets were overshadowed by how fast people where making money in the technology world and in the stock market. But that's why the quick success was not working for everyone; just think about it—how many people were creating innovative world changing products and services that were greatly in demand? So when things fall apart, it's back to the fundamentals, because the basics work. Besides, it takes more than money to grow a business. Some businesses you can even start with very little or no cash, just your skills. But you need a plan, a map of where you are going and the routes you need to take to get there. You need to execute your plan, time to make your business work, and the discipline to do the work. Every business owner is different, everyone's life situation is different, but business principles remain the same, and they will get you results if you understand and apply them the right way to your unique scenario. So, journey with me through these pages as I share with you how to create a profitable business.

PART ONE

THE SOLOPRENEUR STATE OF MIND

LESSONS IN BUSINESS

1

THE BIG PICTURE

"The purpose of every merchant is to make a lawful and reasonable profit so as to keep up his business."

~ LUCA PACIOLI

Merchants. That's what they called them centuries ago when men travelled on foot, horses, camels, and ships to trade goods. The merchants at times endured harsh terrains, weather, and some left their families behind for weeks, months, and even years just to get ahead in life. As the travelling merchants arrived in the various cities for trade, the money changers would receive the merchant's foreign currency and exchange it for the local currency. This made it easier for the merchants to buy and sell goods.

From Africa to the Mediterranean, the sacrifice made to trade goods was nothing compared to the rewards of being financially independent. Today we call them business owners—same concept, same purpose, but different means of accomplishing it. Our worlds are much closer now thanks to technology. Foreign travel only takes a few hours by plane, money is transferred in seconds, and information is certainly in no short supply. But is it the right information? Have you ever wondered, with so many resources why several business owners are still struggling? Why don't we have more self-employed people who are financially independent? Why don't we have more profitable businesses? What's missing? Well, something is certainly missing, and if you've ever wonder the same fret not—you are about to find out why. We will start with the essentials, and then as you read through these pages the mystery will begin to unfold before your eyes. In no time, you'll be well on your way to understanding how to have a profitable business.

WHO'S REALLY SELF-EMPLOYED?

The desire for financial independence inspires many people to explore ways to increase their income. One way to get additional income is through business ownership. For many individuals who want to start their own business, self-employment is the easiest way to start. Self-employment is when you work for yourself; represent yourself in your own business, for your own business and as your own brand. This means that you do the work in order to generate income for the business. Another term for a person who is self-employed is *solopreneur*. As a solopreneur, you alone bear the responsibility of the day-to-day functions of your business, you may have contractors who work for you, you might collaborate with other business owners, or even outsource some of the things you don't want to do, but you shoulder the risk and enjoy the rewards. The U.S. Internal Revenue Service defines self-employment as "anyone who carries on a trade or business as a

Sole Proprietor or an Independent Contractor." A sole proprietor is an individual who owns an *unincorporated* business alone, they may have employees but they are the only owner. The business could be a restaurant, a dry cleaner, an architectural firm or any other business establishment. An independent contractor is an individual that offers their services to the general public, they can be in an independent trade or profession in which they have the right to control and direct the results of their work. Independent contractors include accountants, brokers, veterinarians, subcontractors, realtors, marketing representatives, insurance agents, independent traders, etc.

THE GENERAL IDEA OF BUSINESS

When you start a business, you will have to invest time and money to get your business up and running. For example, if you are going to open a small grocery store a few things you will need to do includes finding a retail location, ordering the merchandise for sale, training employees, marketing the business, and negotiating with vendors to secure get a favorable price on goods and services. Each of these activities requires either time or money to get the business up and running. Once your business has started, it must be maintained and marketed properly in order for it to continue producing income for you. As income is generated, you must manage your expenses wisely in order for the business to become profitable. Expenses are the various cost of running and keeping up a business, such as rent, utilities, licenses, permits, supplies, phone, salaries, and inventory. Once your business is profitable you now have a return on your investment. This return is the earnings you made in excess of the amount you invested into the business to get it up and running. The more sales you make or the more services you provide, the more revenue your business is generating.

For example, assume that you are a social media consultant and you charge $200 per hour for consulting services. If you provide 4 hours of consulting services daily for 5 days per week, you will make $800 per day or $4,000 per week. Likewise, if you provide 6 hours of consulting services daily for 5 days per week, you will make $1,200 per day or $6,000 per week. The more hours of service you provide, the more revenue your business will generate. Further, let's assume that your business expenses are fixed cost totaling $2,000 every month. If you advise clients daily for 4 hours per day for 5 days per week, your monthly income will be about $16,000. Now, when you subtract your monthly expenses of $2,000 your profit will be $14,000. If this was your first month of being in business, and you invested $5,000 of your own money to get the business up and running, then you will consider $9,000 to be your real return on your investment—not bad huh! If your $5,000 investment had been a loan from the bank or a family member, you would pay back the loan and reinvest a portion of the $9,000 back into the business to fund the growth or apply it towards operating cost. The computation for the consulting firm earnings assumptions is shown in figure 1.1.

Daily Earnings:
   (Service fee per hour) x (Number of consulting hours) = Earnings
   $200 x 4 hours = $800
Weekly Earnings:
   (Daily Earnings) x (Number of days worked) = Earnings
   $800 x 5 = $4,000
Monthly Earnings:
   (Weekly Earnings) x (Four weeks) = Earnings
   $4,000 x 4 = $16,000
Monthly Net Profits:
   (Monthly Earnings) – (Expenses) = Profits
   $16,000 - $2,000 = $14,000

Initial Return on Investment:
(Net Profit – Initial Investment) ÷ Initial Investment (($14,000 - $5,000 = $9,000) ÷ $9,000) x 100%= 180%
The 180% means that you made back 100% of your investment, plus an additional 80% on top of that.

Return on Investment is abbreviated ROI, and it shows you how much you made from a specific investment.

Return on Equity:
   (Net Profit ÷ Total Investment) x 100%
   ($14,000 ÷ $5,000) x 100%= 280%

Return on Equity is abbreviated ROE, and it shows how much you made on your individual ownership stake. Net profit is your profit after taxes, and your total investment is the sum of your debt and equity used to fund the business. Using the Accounting Equation total investment is shown below.

Assets =(Liabilities + Owners Equity)

Remember, the sum of your acquired debt to fund the business and the money you personally contributed to the business equals your total investment in the business.

Figure 1.1

Profits from your business can be used towards marketing to attract new customers, used to acquire more inventories for sale, applied towards the purchase of new equipment or invested in technology to help you work more efficiently. These are just a few examples of reinvesting profits back into the business; but your business model which is discussed in chapter three, will serve as an excellent source to help you determine your priorities for growth. Reinvesting profits back into the business is a method of getting your money to make money for you. Many successful business owners who started with very little used this technique to acquire wealth. You may also put a portion of your profits into other investments to generated income from other sources. We will elaborate on the importance of having other sources of income later in chapter seven. It is this act of investing your money (profits) to get it working for you that serves as the key to unlock the door which leads to financial independence. Once the door has been opened, you will have to discipline yourself to continue doing what's required to reach your goals and patiently allow time for your investments to grow. Keep from being distracted by outside influences and concentrate on your work. Do not lose sight of your vision, and maintain a clear understanding of your purpose for taking the various steps to achieve your goals.

THE QUESTION OF PROFITABILITY

So how does a business become profitable? The answer is to spend less than you make; as you generate income you need to keep your expenses low—but achieving it isn't as easy as it sounds. It is the lack control over business expenses that has caused so many self-employed people to stumble and fall on the road to growing their business, and attaining financial independence. Many business owners with the potential to build a thriving business quit out of frustration, not being able to get a handle on their finances they miss the opportunity to see their business flourish. Usually, hiring an accountant can help eliminate that frustration, but some business owners try to handle everything alone to save money and eventually crash.

If you have ever wrestled with thoughts in your mind about how to grow your business and wondered what successful solopreneurs do to turn such high profits, then you are the reason why this book has been written. Nobody likes struggling to get ahead, but so many business owners do. What causes business owners to struggle? The lack knowledge; I believe that if you know what to do, you will do it. Well, if you are serious about getting results, you will do what you must to become successful—right. Several of the business owners who reached out to me for help originally came to me because they had reached a point of desperation. They wanted to know what to do to ensure the survival of their business, and for some business owners they really wanted to avoid getting in trouble with the U.S. Internal Revenue Service (IRS). They wanted peace of mind and the ability to manage their business with confidence.

Usually, the general focus of the average business owner is to make more money and pay less taxes—that's understandable. But imagine operating your business without even knowing how much your net profits truly are, or what you spent most of your money on because you didn't know how to properly organize your books. Sounds farfetched? The truth is; this happens all the time in many businesses. How are you going to become profitable if you keep doing what is not working for you? Some business owners are even living with the fear of being audited because they are not sure if they are operating their business right, a restless mind— that's not healthy. No one should have to run a business with such uncertainties. The reason for these uncertainties is that many business owners don't know what to do, or how to do the things that need to be done. As the saying goes "you don't know what you don't know." This lack of knowledge eventually shows up in the outcomes of the business, success or failure. So don't be unrealistic about it, take the initiative to effect change by educating yourself and implementing the things you have learned.

TREAT YOUR BUSINESS LIKE A BUSINESS

Understanding what business is about and why you are in business is essential to help you to stay focused on your goals. Some people say that business is not about making money, but rather about solving a problem; while others say that business is about making money, and if you see an unmet need you can make that your business—by doing so, you help others and yourself in the process. One thing I know for sure is that if your business is not making money you will not have a business for long. It takes money to run a business, but if you are not meeting a need or solving a problem your business may not be around for long either. You might be thinking "how am I to meet a need or solve a problem? I just want to sell "Ice Cream!" It may sound complicated, but it's not. It means you'll have to identify the benefits of what you are offering and share those benefits with your target market; but you also need to have an idea of what people want or need so that you can cater to them properly.

It is important to understand the process of business, how it grows, how a business is operated, and how it is sustained. In addition, it is also important that you understand your business, how things are done in the industry that you are in. As a self- employed person you are a business owner; and you must begin to see yourself as such and treat your business like a business or you may miss the opportunity before you. Even if you became self-employed because you were looking for a job and never found one so you decided to create work for yourself to survive; or you got an opportunity to make money from a hobby—you are still operating a business. In business your perspective about what is happening, how it's happening and why things are happening will impact your decision making. People make decisions based on what they know, and the results of those choices are insensitive to who you are as a person. Some people say that "what you don't know won't hurt you.", it will hurt you. How many people complain about having worked twenty five years and have nothing to show for it, simply because they did not know about planning for future years' income, never purchased any assets; and did not understand how to go about it. How much of a difference would that piece of information have made in their life?

Make it a priority to understand business principles so that you can maximize the return on your investment in your business. Principles are the basic guidelines and knowledge of business; many were brought forth from the experiences of those who have journeyed on the path that you are currently taking. Other principles were established through the study of the economy over the centuries, as well as insights from religious matters. These principles help keep you from getting yourself into disastrous business situations and they also reduce your learning curve. Many people in business have a particular focus, but do not always understand that there are other things that will impact the end result that they are seeking. For instance, focusing your attention on generating more revenues because you want to have greater profits. But you should also think about steps that must be taken to control your costs and how to allocate the funds for maximum returns. The end result here is greater profits, but what do you do to ensure that you meet those goals? If you don't put into practice the behaviors to see positive changes you'll eventually run into financial difficulties. Regardless of what motivated you into self- employment, you have an opportunity before you. Use this opportunity responsibly and seize this moment to change your financial life.

LESSONS IN BUSINESS

2

TRANSITIONING FROM EMPLOYEE TO SELF-EMPLOYED

"It was character that got us out of bed, commitment that moved us into action, and discipline that enabled us to follow through."

~ ZIG ZIGLAR

Many people start a business while still working full-time as an employee of another company. This is a good time to get a sense of what your customers want, develop your business, and save money before transitioning full-time into the business. However, at some point in order for the business to flourish, you have to take that leap of faith and dive right into the business full-time if you want to take it to the next level. This is because a developing business needs to be nurtured in order for it to grow. It needs to be structured properly, organized, marketed, and funded the right way. Prospective customers need to be educated on the various products and services, and existing customers need to be serviced with care to keep them coming back. In addition, as the business owner you need the experience from working in the business so that you can evaluate areas that need improvements and make the necessary adjustments. All of these tasks require some kind of time commitment and no one does it better than—you! Your vision and passion will serve as the force that moves the business in the right direction.

SMOOTH AND SUCCESSFUL TRANSITIONS

How does one know when it's the right time to transition full time into their business? No one can truly say when to make the move into a business full-time. There is no formula for this, but you can plan to ensure that you have the basics in place to avoid business disruptions. The first of these basics is finances, which is usually the main reason that so many self-employed people struggle. This is a subject not normally discussed enough, but finances need to be assessed before you leave your job for the world of solopreneurship. For many solopreneurs, the struggle does not come primarily from slow revenues, or inadequate savings, but rather poor management of the funds available. On the personal side, instability in the household finances and the pressures of family responsibilities can make launching and growing a business a real big challenge. This is even more prevalent in households where there is only one source of income in the family.

So, how does a person deal with this challenge? Everyone in the family (spouse and children) will have to work as a team to make the dream a reality. Working as a team could be asking for a certain number of hours for quiet time to focus on the business, you could also ask your spouse to help you make some phone calls or ask your teenagers to help with some social media promotions. Therefore, communicating with your family to let them know of your intentions will help them to be prepared and informed about your efforts. It also may serve as an opportunity to teach your children about money and how to use it wisely. Depending on their age, you can get them involved in some of the discussions to get their ideas and feedback on the business. You might be pleasantly surprised how much your children already understand and how they can help make your business better. Further, communication and transparency will help bring to light any concerns, this way issues can be handled appropriately.

Every self-employed person journeyed into business from different walks of life and with access to different levels of resources. Some people were let go from their jobs and although they looked for work elsewhere, no company hired them. Others realized that the only way to attain a better financial life was to become self-employed, yet others sought the freedom to reach their God given potential and excel beyond the limitations set by their jobs. Considering these circumstances it is very unlikely that every solopreneur had adequate funds to start their business. If an individual was not even working before they started their business, then it can probably be said that they had very little or no money when the business was started. But in spite of everything, these types of challenges can be overcome with practical business principles, strategies and good financial management. It does require discipline to make things happen. If you are currently experiencing similar challenges, you are going to have to draw motivation from within you and focus on your goals. Get the required work done in order to see results.

I would like to draw attention to the importance of critical thinking and problem solving skills. Sometimes, it might seem scary transitioning into becoming self-employed fulltime, because it seems like things are not perfectly in place for you to make that transition. Let me help calm your nerves if this is your current position. If you wait for everything to fall into place, you will never move forward because the situation is usually never perfect. Even if you get everything to go just as you want it, once you get into business there is no telling what can emerge unexpectedly. Being able to think critically and solve problems are good skills to develop so that you can assess a situation and act to resolve issues. For example, what do you pay first when you don't have enough money to cover all your expenses? Or, how do you manage your funds when there is a timing difference between when you are getting paid from a client and when your bills are due? Both of these situations can bring on tremendous stress, but if you develop your ability to solve problems analytically you can avoid stressing and act quickly.

FINDING YOUR PATH

Self-employment offers you the opportunity to design the life that you want. It forces you to think differently, beyond what would be considered normal and to explore your creative abilities. It empowers you to grow in knowledge and wisdom, and become the best you can be. It gives you a platform to make a difference in the lives of other people and your community. Around the world, especially in emerging nations entrepreneurship is common because there are not as many large corporations to offer employment. Self-employed people rely on income from farming, owning a local restaurant or store, sewing, operating an auto shop, chauffeuring, and even working as an independent broker or distributor. For many of them self-employment is the only way to survive and thrive, and knowing the principles of running a successful business helps to propel them to a better financial life. If you are certain about self-employment but concerned about finances, you may want to consider working part-time elsewhere and fulltime in your business this way you can build your business and avoid financial hardship. This solution will demand a bit more of your time, but it will give you the ability to plan a transition strategy that will offer you peace of mind. Table 2.1 shows some differences between a self-employed person and an employee.

Table 2.1 Differences between self-employed and employed

Activity	Employee	Self-employed
Decision Making	Follow company predetermined rules.	Think for yourself, make a decision, and act on it.
Hours worked	Clock–in and Clock–out.	Put in the needed time to get the work done.
Healthcare and Retirement Benefits	Various affordable options, but limited to what the company chooses to offer.	Healthcare cost can be very high, but there are options. Retirement is covered by planning and allocating business income wisely to the many retirement options strategically.
Resources	Just make a request, may need approval.	Get what you can afford when you need it.
Mentoring	Ask for guidance, often provided as part of the company standards.	Take initiatives to educate yourself, seek help through chambers, motivational CDs and DVDs, Books and other industry experts.

Income		
	Steady paycheck, but limited income potential. In addition, employees get what's left after taxes, benefits, and other obligations are deducted.	Could go months without pay, can also earn thousands or even millions. Ability to transition into passive income. Can decide when and how to use all income received.
Taxes	Company pays for a portion of taxes and withholds employees estimated tax obligation.	Business owner is responsible for all taxes due, but can apply tax laws to pay lower taxes.
Job Security	No guarantee of employment.	Unlimited opportunity, it depends on the individual's motivation.
Job Scope	Focus on assigned task.	Self-employed persons wears many hats, caring out most of the functions in the earlier years, but can hire help when needed.

Some people hesitate making the transition into self-employment because of the paralyzing emotion called fear. At the root of fear is the lack of confidence in being accepted by the marketplace and in being successful in business. In other words, people hesitate making the transition into self-employment because of the fear of rejection and failure. The marketplace is a competitive one and most of the time the entities with a good marketing plan and focus survive. While marketing and staying focus are keys to reaching business goals, many consumers these days are looking beyond the publicity and zeroing in on authenticity and quality. They are looking for businesses that care about their customers, as well as their products and services. Such passion is reflected naturally by the value added services rendered and in the quality of the work produced. Fear has caused so many unemployed, yet talented people, to go years without work because they are waiting for someone to rescue them with a job offer. If they are not offered a job, they assume that there is something wrong with them, and out of desperation to keep their livelihood, they take a minimum wage job. I have spoken with several highly educated college graduates who go years from one minimum wage paying job to the next, and when I offer suggestions to them about how to put their knowledge to work they simply give me that look of uncertainty. The purpose of education appears to have changed. It used to be about becoming a well–rounded individual, but now many people go to school for the specific purpose of finding a job, even if it's in an area that they are not interested. Education does open the door for opportunity, but when things fall apart why not use those skills learned in the four to eight years of higher education to chart your own course. If you never got a college education it should not stop you either, no one ever inquires about your college transcript before giving you a loan or deciding to use your services. Besides, you can always fund your own education with your business profits and study what you really want and be more fulfilled.

Everyone has a skill that they are good at, even if it's seasonal services. Instead of sitting home feeling sorry about your life, be strong and have courage to do the work because everyone has unique abilities given from God, and since He gave it to you there must be a need somewhere. Figure out what you need to do, where the needs are, if you must, move to another city or country and build your business there. Take control of your life, don't put it in the hands of another person—listen, no person has it all together. When you were a child, naturally people (Parents or Guardian) had control over you, but now that you are an adult your God-given life is your responsibility. Take ownership and do something great for yourself.

Listed in table 2.2 are 120 amazing low to no cost self-employment start-up ideas. Many of these services can be offered to businesses and individuals, note that licensing requirements may vary by state, city or country.

THINK AND ACT LIKE A SOLOPRENEUR

The mindset of an employee is very different from that of a self- employed person because of their focus. Just think back to when you were an employee or think of your current job if you are still working. Your focus was not on how to generate revenues for the company or controlling the business expenses. Your focus was on exceeding performance expectations, meeting quotas, and doing your job right. As such, the skills that were being developed were the ones essential to being more efficient and effective at the job you were hired to do. As a self-employed person you will now have to transition your mind and behaviors to think and act like the business person that you are. You will have to start developing your business skills so that you can maximize your potential. One of the business skills you will have to develop is the ability to work at your business. As an employee you have to go above and beyond the basic expectations in order to be a star employee. What if you applied those same behaviors that made you a valued employee at your job to your own business, How far could you take your business? How much could you get accomplished each day if you disciplined yourself? How much income could you generate? If you apply the same dedication and excellent work ethics to your own business, you can change your life. Of course, you can change your life! It's your business and the success of your business means that you will reap the financial rewards. So go ahead, make the transition, and eliminate the fear of failure by planning and working your plan. If it is possible, also set aside some emergency money to cover your business expenses. These suggestions are very good ways you can transition confidently into your business full-time without the fear of failure.

Dream it, Plan it, Do it!

What are some of the challenges preventing you from transitioning into or starting your business?

_____

_____

_____

What are some steps you can take to overcome these challenges?

_____

_____

_____

How will the success of your business change your life?

_____

_____

_____

Take Action

If you are currently unemployed, write down two or three self-employment opportunities you believe you can do. Then using the internet, research the requirements needed to get started. Get excited and get moving!

_____

_____

_____

Table 2.2 Low to no cost start-up ideas

1. Commercial Cleaning	36. Writer /Blogger/Columnist
2. Residential Cleaning	37. PR Services
3. Local Publication	38. Freelance Transcriptions
4. Printing Services	39. Freelance Editing
5. Car Wash	40. Legal Transcriptions
6. Mobile Car Detailing	41. Translator
7. Mobile Laundry Delivery	42. Online Book Store
8. Blind Cleaning	43. Online Party Supply Store
9. Food Truck	44. Online Consignment Store
10. Catering	45. Drop-ship E-commerce Store
11. Home-Based Bakery	46. Create/ Sell Arts and Craft Online
12. Home Health Services	47. Restaurant Equipment Repair
13. Tutoring Services (*math, foreign language, accounting, etc.*)	48. Computer Repair
14. Carpet Cleaning	49. Auto Repair
15. Tile and Grout Cleaning	50. Windshield, Rim, Wheel Repair
16. House Clean-Outs (*for property managers and realtors*)	51. Furniture Repair
17. Landscaping	52. Pool Repair
18. Lawn Care	53. Roofing Repair
19. Pest Control	54. Foundation Repair
20. Junk removal	55. Plummer
21. Window Washing	56. Electrician
22. Pool Cleaning	57. Bath and Kitchen Remodeling
23. DJ Services	58. Power Washing Services (*roofs, concrete floors, etc.*)
24. Party Supply Rentals	59. Flooring Installation and Restoration
25. Gift Wrapping Services	60. Handyman Services
26. Children's Party Planner	61. Valet Parking
27. Corporate Party Planner	62. Web Designer
28. Wedding Planner	63. Painting Services
29. Events Planner	64. Property Management
30. Travel Planner	65. Booking Agent
31. Local Tour Guide	66. Personal Concierge Service
32. Events Photographer	67. Fashion Consultant
33. Photojournalist	68. Seamstress/Tailoring Services
34. Freelance Illustrator	69. Mobile Hair Salon
35. Social Media Specialist	

70. Massage Therapist	95. Computer/Software Trainer
71. Counseling	96. Virtual Assistant/Secretary
72. Makeup Artist (*weddings, proms, quinceañeras, sweet sixteen, fashion shows, etc.*)	97. Virtual Call Center Agent
	98. Professional Organizer
	99. Graffiti Removal Services
73. Child Care services	100. Commercial Inspector
74. Tennis Coach	101. Residential Inspector
75. Football Coach	102. Appraiser
76. Swimming Instructor	103. Residential Realtor
77. Fitness Class Instructor	104. Commercial Realtor
78. Personal Fitness Trainer	105. Home Stager
79. Children Fitness	106. Interior Designer-Commercial
80. Dance Instructor	107. Interior Designer-Residential
81. Nutritionist	108. Freelance Landscape Designer
82. Dog Walker	109. Freelance Architect
83. Pet Grooming	110. Auction Lister
84. In-Home Veterinarian Services	111. Packing Services
85. Garage Sales Specialist	112. Fence and Gate Installer (*residential, commercial*)
86. Bookkeeping Service	113. Security Installation services
87. Accounting Services	114. Event Security Services
88. Tax Services	115. Local Tour Guide Services
89. Gymnastics Coach	116. Chauffeur Services
90. Cheerleading Coach	117. Subcontractor
91. Voice and Music Instructor	118. Tree Trimming Services
92. Pageant Consultant	119. Nail Technician (*can also contract with podiatrist*)
93. Private Chef	120. Grill Cleaning and Repair
94. Local Moving Services	

PART TWO

MAKING YOUR VISION A REALITY

LESSONS IN BUSINESS

3

MAKING YOUR BUSINESS WORK

"Planning is bringing the future into the present
so that you can do something about it now."

~ ALAN LAKEIN

Every self-employed person wants their business to work, but figuring out which pieces to connect at times is a challenge. When a business owner who's facing a challenge begins to think that there's no way to overcome it, frustration sets in and the business may begin to feel like a burden. Sometimes business owners do not even realize that this frustration is causing them to make poor decisions, which can lead to more problems or make a situation worst. Another observation worth noting is that when a person starts to feel like they are losing control, in the heat of the moment, there is a tendency to overlook all learned principles and their natural reaction for handling a situation takes over. This reaction is not always the best course of action, because what's triggering the reaction most of the time is *anxiety*, which is an emotion. Desperation, fear, embarrassment, confusion, and uncertainty are a few examples of emotions that may lead to irrational reactions.

To help solopreneurs stay focused on their purpose and avoid being distracted from their goals, there's a set of documents that every self- employed business owner needs to have. These documents are very useful in helping self-employed individuals see the bigger picture so that strategic plans can be put in place to help them achieve their business goals, and to help identify areas in the business that need to be worked on. The reason these documents are recommended, is because many solopreneurs usually think that they have a very good idea of how they want their business structured and what it will take to be successful. But quickly realize that they have not considered all the factors that may impact the success of their business once it has been put on paper. While you can never predict the future, you can apply proven strategies for success shared by successful entrepreneurs who have already achieved what you are trying to achieve.

PUTTING YOUR DREAMS INTO A PLAN

In this section, we will take a look at the most crucial of these documents and reveal why they are so important. These documents help to make up what is known as a *Business Plan*, they are also a guide to help you determine what your *Operating Plan* will be. Just to clarify, our focus is on the most essential documents, these are the articles you will need to get you moving towards profitability, once your business is a little more established you will have a better understanding of where you want your business to be years from now, and able to put together a business plan. If you want to have a profitable business, start writing down what you want to accomplish with your business and where you would like it to be one, two, and three years from now. Once you have determined these, put together a strategy to help you reach those goals. However, because unforeseen events are inevitable, be prepared to adjust your course from time to time—but keep your focus on your destination. The misunderstanding over the years has been that these documents were only needed if a business owner wanted a loan from a bank or an investor in their business. Reality is that these documents are for you, the business owner, so that you can be successful in business. Further, if it so happens that you need a loan or an investor, then the likelihood of you receiving financial support will be increased. This is because your prospective investors or lenders will see how carefully you have planned the success of your business.

It may take some time for you to organize your thoughts and put your ideas, goals, and business purpose in writing, but a little bit of time invested in this blueprint will help you to capture all the elements that your business will need in order for it to grow and be successful. This method of planning has been useful over the years to help business owners stay on course. An added advantage is that your plans will be available as a reference for you when you need to check yourself to ensure that decisions are in line with your business purpose. Such as, planning your yearly and quarterly financial goals or determining what marketing channels will work best for your needs. As your business evolves or customers provide you with feedback, you can modify these plans to be relevant and reflect the current goals of your business. We will go through each one to help you broaden your understanding of them so you can put together your own guidance package. As you begin to put these plans together keep in mind that they are for you, so it does not need to be long and drawn out. All you need is well-thought- out ideas about where your business is heading, and how you plan to get there expressed in both qualitative and quantitative formats. Quantitative refers to measurable information such as financial information, while the qualitative information focuses on who, what, where, when, how and why of the plans. Let's take a look at the first of these crucial reports.

Your Business Model

Have you ever thought about how you are going to market your business? How you are going to attract customers to buy your products? Have you ever wondered how those big businesses and famous entrepreneurs always seem to know exactly what to do to make money? Well, it did not happen as easily as it appears. Of course they do some marketing, but there was something else they did before they figured out the right marketing formula. It started with the draft of a Business Model, and then they tested it to see if it was effective in getting them the results they wanted. If the model did not work they designed another one and continued to tweak it until they found the formula that worked. Some of these business models where already being used by business owners in the various industries, so new startups simply selected a few from the already proven methods within their industry. Once they identified the best one, they applied the model to their business. Of course, with some minor changes in order to custom fit it to their own business, and they too began to see growth. Finding the right marketing technique can be one of the most challenging aspects of running a business for self-employed people. Primarily because it can take quite a bit of money to employ the right marketing at times, and many solopreneurs cannot afford it. Instead, many self- employed people rely on organic methods to build their businesses, but without having the right business model, this too can be expensive and ineffective. To avoid wasting money, business owners can test their marketing strategy to determine which ones are most effective in getting results. For example, having the same words on two print advertisements with each showing a different picture. The testing in this example is to see which one gets the best response. Another test could be figuring out whether social media or radio advertising gets you the best response. There are several cost effective marketing methods, and we will examine these further in chapter seven.

What exactly is a Business Model?

A business model is your profit plan. It is a blueprint of how your business is going to create value for your customers and how you plan to generate cash flow from proving the valued services or products to your customers. You can design your own business model from scratch, buy the software, or hire a business model design company to do the research and design one for you. But, being a solopreneur it may be more cost effective to design your own. Your business model shows how your company plans on creating value for your customers, who you are targeting, the channels you are going to use to deliver that value to your targeted customers, any partners that will be used to help you reach your goals, how you plan to sustain and grow the business, what makes your business unique, and how you plan to make money from meeting the customers' needs. It should also include what it will cost you to carry out these efforts and what strategies you plan to use to make your plan work. Once your business model is complete it will be easier for you to plan out your marketing efforts.

When you have your business model, or a least a good model to put to the test, then you can decide which marketing methods and service providers you are going to use. For example, if you decide to open a bakery, will the bakery just be a local bakery? Will the bakery target pastry and coffee drinkers? Who are your customers; business people or will you target wedding and birthday clients? Will you have an online store that will receive orders and ship it to customers in other cities or states? What will your primary form of delivery be? Will you ship directly from your bakery or will you partner with a supplier bakery who will personalize orders with your logo and information? How will customers find you and buy from you? How much are you going to charge and why? Is your pricing justified by the value you are offering? And based on your decisions, what will be the best marketing channel to reach your targeted customers? These are just a few things that go into putting together your business model. Once you have figured all of this out, making a decision on some of the other business needs will be a much easier.

Below is a general business model in figure 3.1 reflecting the order of thinking that goes into setting up a prototype for a business.

The business model is sometimes referred to as your profit formula. Your business model needs to capture the essential cost of delivering value to your customers. Value, is the perceived effect of your product or service to your customer in helping them improve their situation or meeting their goals. Higher value in many cases justifies the reason for the price you are charging.

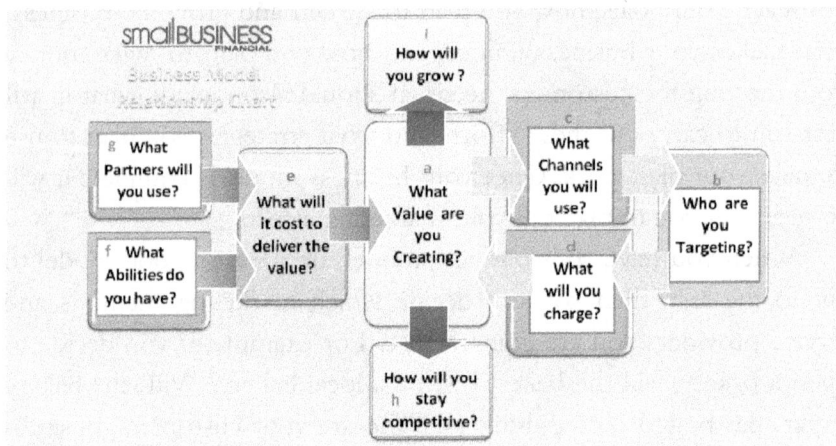

Figure 3.1 Business model chart.

- Box (a) represents your starting point; here you must first determine what value you are creating.

- Boxes (b), (c) and (d) represent your profit factory, how you will deliver the value to your customers, and how your business will make money from proving this value.

- Boxes (e), (f) and (g) represent the cost of being able to deliver these services or value to your target customers. You may have cost incurred from maintain partners, hiring experts, employees or contractors to help your business achieve results. Also, you may incur cost from implementing technology like building a website or subscribing to a service.

- Boxes (h) and (i) represent how you plan to maintain your business share in the marketplace and grow it.

Your business model is a great starting point to help you get your business up and running in the right direction. Depending on your industry and the specifics of what you will be offering, you may be able start your business simply with a good business model and your business essentials; then develop the other plans as you get a sense of what customers want, what the economy is like or will be, and the developments in your industry.

As you design your business model, it will force you to think about other key areas that will need to be expanded on later, such as your financial plan, your marketing plan and your operating plan.

How do I determine my cost and sales price?

To figure out how much you will charge for services you can use one of two common pricing methods. Value Based Pricing and Cost-Plus pricing, they are not the only price methods but they are widely used in the business world. Value based pricing is a method in which prices are determined based on the value that the service or products provides to the customer. For example, a mobile phone with certain features may be perceived to be more valuable because of the convenience it offers its users, so because of this value customers are willing to pay a premium for the particular phone. Cost-Plus pricing on the other hand is a pricing method in which the cost of the product or service is first determined and then a markup is added to it to arrive a selling price.

With cost-plus pricing all cost to provide the product or service is broken into fixed cost and variable cost. Fixed cost are cost that remain constant regardless of the level of activity in a business. So when making a product, these cost usually remain the same for the business year. For example, rent, salaries, marketing and other administrative cost are all examples of fixed cost, and they usually stay the same for the entire business year. It may be easier to think of fixed cost as those cost which have been budgeted for and will not change from month to month whether you sell, produce or add a new business product or not. Variable cost, these cost will change in proportion to the level of activity in a business. For example, if you buy baskets used in putting together gift sets for your clients from another company, then you will probably order them in large amounts to get better pricing. Let's assume one hundred baskets for a total price of $100.00, that's $1.00 per basket or per unit. Now if you add an additional fifty baskets to the original order, the supplier may now charge a different price. Let's assume that the new total price will be $125.00, this equates to $0.83 per basket or per unit. The price per unit for the baskets change as more baskets are ordered, this is an example of a variable cost. Fixed costs are great because you can easily determine your markup and profit better for the business year. But variable costs are a little more challenging, because it depends on the level of production.

When using cost plus pricing you must figure out the per unit cost of a product or per hour cost of a service. In retail or manufacturing businesses there may be more variable cost than fixed as supposed to a service industry, like a consulting firm. In a retail business, you can figure out the cost of each unit of product being sold by looking at what you paid for it, as in the example above ($125 ÷ 150 baskets = $0.83 per basket). If you were charged shipping and handling make sure you add it into the total cost before computing the actual per unit cost. For manufacturers, there is a price for every item used to make a product, so take the total cost to make the product and divide it by the quantity that it will be allocated to. For example, if you are a chef catering an event with one hundred people attending and you figure that a ten pound bag of white rice costing $5.00 will be enough. Variable cost is determined by taking the total cost divided by the plates produced. $5.00 ÷ 100 = $0.05 per plate. Variable cost is usually the cost directly incurred in making a product, and it includes material and labor cost. So, if you have someone on your team making the rice, your total cost will include their wages for the event.

Dream it, Plan it, Do it!

1. *What services or products will you offer in the marketplace?*

    _____

    _____

    _____

2. *What value will these services or product provide to your customers?*

    _____

    _____

    _____

3. *What value do you bring to the marketplace?*

    _____

    _____

    _____

4. *What benefits will customers receive from using your products or services?*

    _____

    _____

    _____

5. *How will you deliver those services or products?*

    _____

    _____

    _____

Take action

- Determine and implement a model for your business that will allow you to make money from the services or products you are offering. Keep in mind that the greater the value you are giving to your customers, the more they may be willing to pay. However, keeping prices relatively the same in a market where there are several people doing what you do may be better to stay competitive. But you may be able to capture market share by offering greater value, even if there are many other businesses like yours in your area. Use the business model chart in this book as a guide or template to help you make sure that all the essential areas of your business model are covered. Be as detailed as possible and do as much research as needed to get answers to unknown questions. The internet is a great place to start your search, also industry regulatory sites, community colleges, universities, and your city government's business development sites may have information or links to where you can get some of the answers you are looking for.

- When using the business model sample in this book to help you design your own, start by answering in details the questions in the business model. You can use a separate page to answer each question, and then summarize your answers on to a draft design of your business model. If you think you've got something special, let your creativity show, you may just bring forth something innovative.

- Also, research to see if you can find types of business models that will be suitable for your business, then analysis them to see the common thread that seems to work in that industry.

Your Marketing Plan

Marketing your business is crucial to getting your business to work. If you want to generate revenue you will have to advertise what you do so that people will know. How you publicize your business will depend on whether you are providing a service or selling products, and who you are seeking to offer these services or products to. In addition, you want to consider the current trends in the marketplace, whether there's a demand for your products or services and why, how to stand out from others who do what you do, and what other services and products your prospective customers are using. Start by determining which category of self-employed you fall under, then see if you can come up with a few examples of other businesses or people who are offering your same service. Table 3.1 shows some known vocations that solopreneurs may operate under, use the chart as a guide to determine where you may fit. Once you have identified businesses similar to yours, do some research to see how they are advertising their business, what media channels they are using, what events they participate in and how they position themselves in the industry. The purpose of the activity is not to copy what they do, but to get an idea of what works in the industry as a way to be seen and heard. Also, this activity will help you get a better understanding of what makes you different or what's unique about your products even if you decide to market your business in a similar way.

At times you may find that there are several people offering the same services that you are offering, so setting yourself apart will require a little more work on your part. But determining what marketing works well in your industry will be easier because all you need to do is observe what the top players in the industry are doing. Sometimes you will find that consumers who use a particular product or service will also use sister products and services, so you may want to consider advertising your business in those markets also. For example, if you are an interior designer you may benefit from advertising to builders, remodeling contractors, painters, including commercial and residential realtors, instead of just individuals as this will broaden your market reach. If you are not sure about what your sister services and products are, pick up an industry magazine to see who's advertising in it. Also, watch industry television shows to see what companies sponsor them or run advertisements during that programing, attend an industry related event, lunch and learns, mixers or conference and see who shows up. If you can't attend the events watch their videos online. Sometimes they upload videos of past events, take a few minutes to observe what's happening. Your marketing plan should be a detail layout of how you plan to promote, package and deliver your services or products to your target consumers.

Table 3.1 Vocational categories of solopreneurs

Business Domain	You promote yourself, you are the brand, you sell your products.	You promote yourself, you are the brand, you sell your services.	You promote a product(s), you sell other companies products.	You promote a service(s), you sell other companies services.
Freelancer	Artists, Musicians, Authors, Jewel Designer Fashion Designers, etc.	Writers, Editors, Interior Designers, Stylist, Bookkeepers, Recruiters, Speakers, etc.	Network Marketers, Dealers, Jewelers, Various Sales Agents, etc.	Network Marketers, Financial Services Agents, etc.
Contractor		Plumbers, Surveyors, Painters, Appraisers, etc.	Actors, Athletes, Medical Equipment Agents, etc.	

Professional		Architects, Doctors, Accountants, Lawyers, Engineers, etc.	Insurance. Agents, Realtors, Call Center. Agents, Investment Advisors, etc.	

Your Financial Plan

While your marketing plan will help you determine how you will bring revenue into your business; your financial plan will help you determine your current and future funding needs, as well as expected income in the future. Money is a very uncomfortable topic for many people to discuss because it is sometimes a window into their personal life as well. Many self-employed people manage their business in a way that accommodates their personal spending needs. For example, most self- employed people live directly off every dollar of profit generated by the business, because there's not enough revenue coming into the business to allocate a monthly salary or draw to the business owner for living expenses. Sometimes there's too much debt in the business, as such the business owner will just live off what's left instead of taking a structured fixed payment. Solopreneurs who have a spouse with a steady income from employment are usually able to work in the business without paying themselves for the first couple of years allowing business profits to be reinvested into the business.

Now, if you are a business owner whose household income is exclusively from your business, make sure that you properly plan for your personal income. Determine the cost of your basic living expenses and include that amount in your business operating budget, then increase your sales revenue goals so that you can plan to bring in enough money to pay yourself a monthly fixed income. When you include it in your business operating budget identify it as labor or salary cost, even if you take an Owners draw include it in your budget. It is common for business owners to forego income for the benefit of growing the business, but this is only temporary. Imagine if every self-employed person was able to reinvest their business profits into their business, we would have financially strong businesses across the world. Financiers would be paid in a timely manner reducing the overall cost of debt, investors would get their returns, there would be money to grow the business, owners would be able to get the right technology and enhance the consumer's experience, credit scores would be higher, businesses would be able to create more jobs because of business growth, the list could go on. What we have instead are self- employed individuals who are challenged with balancing their business and personal financial life, struggling to manage their money and turn a profit. Solutions for managing your business and personal finances are addressed later.

The power of the financial plan

Have you ever considered how much you could make in your business? What's that figure? Many self-employed people underestimate the power of planning. What hinders people from reaching their goals is the lack of planning and discipline in carrying out their plans. Lots of people dream of a better future, being financially independent and able to live the life they want. But few people ever do something about it, and several others never learned how to achieve goals. If you are one of the few that never learned how to achieve goals, you perhaps have found yourself journeying to success without a proper road map. This means you took a few wrong turns, ran into some road blocks, detoured and hoped that you make it to the right destination. You also probably made some progress, but not at the rate you wanted. Well, what if you could predict your future earnings, how much would you choose to make? Whatever that number is write it down. Begin to design a practical plan on how you intend to make it happen and by faith start doing the things that should be done so that you can achieve your goals.

Design your *Financial Plan.* Your financial plan is a forecast of where you think (or would like) your business will be financially in the coming three to five years. Before you design your financial plan you need to be realistic about the current financial state of your business, which is a reflection of how you have been running your business. The current financial state of your business will be reflected in your financial statements, this is your *Balance Sheet*, Income Statement commonly referred to as *Profit and Loss*, and the *Cash Flow* statement. These statements reflect history, how well your business has done so far to date. To help you reach your goals you will need (a) an *Operating Budget* which is your spending guide and (b) A three or five year *financial projection* to help you plan for your future financial goals. These are the essential parts of your financial plan, and your mission is to create and use these plans as a road map to help you accomplish your financial goals. In addition, you must create an action plan indicating how you plan to reach the projected numbers and then work that plan. To help you monitor your progress, you will need performance measures to evaluate how you are doing every month.

Dream it, Plan it, Do it!

YOUR OBJECTIVES

- Design a three or five year income projection of where you would like your business to be financially.

- Create an operating budget that will serve as your monthly spending guide.

- Use the three essential financial statements to help you determine the financial health of your business; and what areas you need to work on in the business to achieve financial results. Analysis tools will be listed below.

GETTING STARTED

A good starting point for your financial projection will be to take your cost of goods and sales price information from your business model and expand on it using your prior year profit and loss statement. If you are newly self-employed, you can either estimate what your revenues and expenses will be in the future based on your experience in the industry or research what the standard ratios are in your industry to help you determine what yours should be. Let's get started, you will first figure out how much you need to sell to cover cost, and then you will add in your desired profit. This will help you determine how much you need to sell to make a profit in current year and future years.

Determine your Break-Even point

Your Break-Even point tells you how many products or services you need to sell to cover all cost. At break-even point you have no losses and no profit.

1. Determine the cost of your services or products. Add up all the cost that went into buying the product for sale or manufacturing it. If you are in the service industry it will be what it cost you to provide the service.

2. Add your mark up. You can use industry averages or shop other businesses similar to yours to see what they are charging as a guide. Be realistic, check for both high and low price ranges then see where your business fits.

Break-Even Calculation:

a) Determine your Contribution Margin (CM). This is what you will have available to allocate towards all your *fixed* cost. Think of fixed cost as your budgeted *administrative and selling* expenses. Examples include rent, marketing and office supplies. Fixed cost remain the same regardless of how many products you make or buy. These costs should be budgeted for to help you keep your business expenses under control. Your *variable* cost are the cost to acquire the products you sell or make, these cost change in proportion to the level of production or purchases for each item being acquired or made. Variable cost is the cost of goods you sell or services you provide.

CM = Sales price per unit – Variable Cost per unit.

Break-Even = Your Total Fixed Cost ÷ CM

Therefore, if you determine that it cost you $10 to make or acquire each product you will sell and you have a mark-up of 50% your selling price is then $15.00 per unit sold. This does not mean your profit is 50% just that you will sell it for 50 % above your cost. Now assume that you completed your operating budget, and you determined that it will cost you $10,000 in administrative and selling expenses for the whole year—your calculation for Break-Even will be the following:

CM: $15.00 - $10 = $5.00

Break Even: $10,000 ÷ $5.00 = 2,000 units

This means that you will have to sell 2,000 units or hours of service to cover all cost in the business for the year. But to make a profit you will have to estimate how much you would like to make, and then add that number to the total fixed cost, and then divide it by your contribution margin to get the number units or hours needed to reach that profit amount. This is known as a *Cost-Volume Profit* analysis (CVP).

b) Determine Cost-Volume Profit analysis (CVP). Let's say you have determined that you want to generate $50,000 for the year in profits. Your calculation based on the figures above will be as follows:

Cost-Volume Profit:

(Desired Profit + Total Fixed Cost) ÷ Contribution Margin per unit.

CVP: ($50,000 + $10,000) ÷ $5.00 = 12,000 units

This means you will have to sell 10,000 additional units or a total of 12,000 for the year in order to make $50,000 in profit for the year. Once you have figured out your desired profit, implement a marketing action plan to make it happen. This is the scientific formula behind the numbers; you must plan and then work your plan.

For Multiple Products

If you have more than one product, to determine your contribution margin for break-even and target profit units, use the *weighted average* of your product sales price and your variable cost— allocate each product according to whatever their percentage make- up towards your total sales usually is or will be. See example below.

a) Determine the weighted average sales price:
Table 3.2 Computing sales price using weighted average method

Sales Mix	Sale Price (Per Unit)	Percent contributed to total Sales	Weighted Average Sales Price
Basket Balls	$ 20.00	40%	$ 8.00
Tennis Balls	$ 10.00	35%	$ 3.50
Footballs	$ 15.00	25%	$ 3.75
Total Sales		100.0%	$ 15.25

b) Determine the weighted average variable cost:

Table 3.3 Computing variable cost using weighted average method

Sales Mix	Variable Cost (Per Unit)	Percent contributed to total Sales	Weighted Average Variable Cost
Basket Balls	$ 10.00	40%	$ 4.00
Tennis Balls	$ 5.00	35%	$ 1.75
Footballs	$ 7.50	25%	$ 1.88
Total VC		100.0%	$ 7.63

CM: $15.25 - $7.63 = $7.62

Break Even: $10,000 ÷ $7.62 = 1,312 units

CVP: ($50,000 + $10,000) ÷ $7.62 = 7,874 units

We can check our math accuracy by itemizing the facts:
Estimated Gross Sales: $15.25 x 7,874 = $120,078
Cost of Production: $7.63 x 7,874 = $60,078
Administrative Costs: $10,000
Profit: $120,078 - $60,078 - $10,000 = $50,000
The numbers may vary by a few pennies.

Create Your Operating Budget

There is no better tool to provide you with guidance on managing the day-to-day operations of your business like your operating budget. Your budget will help you identify expected revenue and whether you have enough coming in to cover anticipated expenses. For example, if you discover that forty percent of your current month's sales revenue will not be collected until the following month, your operating budget will help you manage your available operating funds wisely. This now gives you a chance to work out a plan to ensure that all your business expenses are paid.

1. Using your prior month's profit and loss statement as a guide, estimate how much revenue you think you will generate for the current month and put it on your budget sheet. Then determine how much your administrative and selling expenses will be and include it in the budget.

2. If you are setting up your operating budget from scratch, you can set it up using any spreadsheet of your choice. The spreadsheet should mirror your profit and loss statement. Your estimated revenues minus your budgeted expenses will tell you what your planned profit will be. Be sure to title your spreadsheet "Operating Budget"

3. Your operating budget should be planned for the entire year, then broken down for the twelve months of the year and monitored on a monthly basis. Be realistic with your estimated revenues and expenses, use this opportunity to evaluate what costs you should keep, eliminate, or reduce. If you find out that you will not be collecting some of your revenue until the next month, look at your budget to see if you will have enough to cover your expenses. If you will not have enough to cover expenses, implement a strategy to ensure that what needs to be paid gets paid—payment strategies are discussed in chapter eight. This is your business and you are the captain of the ship

so direct it in the direction you want it to go. If a supplier is costing you too much money, then start shopping for better pricing with another supplier or negotiate with your existing supplier for a better rate.

Create Your Income Projection

As noted previously, financial statements reflect the history of your business transactions. It shows how much you generated in revenues, what you invested your money in, what expenses you incurred, money you borrowed and how much of your own money you personally invested in the business. For further insights you can run some financial analysis to evaluate your business performance. *Horizontal analysis* is used to analyze trends in the financial statement, such as determining which expenses have increased in the past year or two and by what percent, or how much has revenue increased compared to the prior year. *Vertical analysis* treats each item on the statement as a percentage of a base. For example, on the income statement, sales revenue can be the base and every item would be a percent of sales.

The vertical analysis can be used to monitor your business performance in any operating period. The purpose of running these analyses is to understand what happened in the operations of business, and why it happened so that you can keep doing them or take corrective action in order to accomplish your business objectives. Table 3.4 provides a simple example of a vertical analysis, and table 3.5 provides a simple example of a horizontal analysis.

a)   Vertical Analysis:

Table 3.4 Computing vertical analysis

Vertical Analysis	Year	Percent of sales
Sales Revenue	$ 100,000	100%
Cost of goods sold	$ 45,000	45%
Gross Profit	$ 55,000	55%
Expenses	$ 35,000	35%
Net income	$ 20,000	20%

a)   This vertical analysis reveals that cost of goods sold were 45% of total sales, determined as follows:

$45,000 ÷ $100,000 = 45%

If this cost were to be more than what you budgeted for, you will need to determine why and implement action steps to reduce your costs.

b)   Horizontal Analysis:

Table 3.5 Computing horizontal analysis

Horizontal Analysis	Current Year	Prior Year	Increase or Decrease	Percent Increase or Decrease
Sales Revenue	$ 100,000	$ 98,000	$ 2,000	2.0%
Cost of goods sold	$ 45,000	$ 38,000	$ 7,000	18.4%
Gross Profit	$ 55,000	$ 60,000	$ (5,000)	-8.3%
Expenses	$ 35,000	$ 37,000	$ (2,000)	-5.4%
Net income	$ 20,000	$ 23,000	$ (3,000)	-13.0%

b) This Horizontal analysis reveals that cost of goods sold increased by $7,000 which is an 18.4% increase from last year, determined as follows:

($45,000 - $38,000) ÷ $38,000

This rise in cost may be a result of poor planning since revenues only increased by 2% for the year or it could be that there was a rise in supplier cost during the year. If this were to be the case then you will need to take corrective action to lower your cost.

Other Tools

Other recommended tools useful in measuring business performance and risk are ratios. Listed below are the three primary types of ratios.

Profitability Ratios: These ratios are useful in evaluating the operating effectiveness of your business. They reveal how profitable your business is, and how well you are using your business assets to turn a profit in any given period.

Common Profitability Ratios:

- *Gross Profit* ratio tells for each dollar of sales revenue the percent available to apply towards all other business cost after cost of goods sold is covered.

  Gross Profit Ratio = Gross Profit ÷ Net Sales

- *Return on Assets* shows how well your business is using its assets (cash, inventory, supplies, equipment, etc.), it indicates for each dollar of asset how much profit you generated.

Return on Assets = Net Income ÷ Average Total Assets

- *Profit Margin* shows for each dollar of sale how much was actual profit.

Profit Margin = Net Income ÷ Net Sales

Average Total Assets is determined by taking the total assets for the current year plus the total assets for the prior year and dividing the results by 2.

(Total Assets Year 1 + Total Assets Year 2) ÷ 2

Liquidity Ratios: These ratios measure your business ability to pay those liabilities that will be due in a year or less, also known as current liabilities.

Common Liquidity Ratios:

- *Current Ratio* reveals whether your business has enough current assets to pay your current debts. A ratio of greater than one means that you have more than enough to cover your monthly expenses.

Current Ratio = Current Assets ÷ Current Liabilities

- *Receivables Turnover* shows how quickly you turn your accounts receivables (A/R) from credit sales into cash. If this ratio is high, then you are good at collecting the money owed to you from credit sales.

Receivables Turnover = Net Credit Sales ÷ A/R.

- *Inventory Turnover* indicates on an average, how many times you had to restock inventory after it was sold. A high turnover ratio means that you are selling your merchandise.

Inventory Turnover = Cost of Goods Sold ÷ Ending Inventory

Debt Ratios: These ratios reveal if your business can pay its long term debt. Formally known as Solvency Ratios, these ratios are useful for showing how much of your assets are financed by debt.

Common Debt Ratios:

- *Debt to Equity* ratio tells whether your business has enough equity to cover all debts of the business.

  Debt to Equity Ratio = Total Liabilities ÷ Owners Equity

- *Times Interest Earned* tells whether your business has enough income available to pay for the interest on a loan.

  Times Interest Earned = Net Income ÷ Interest Expense

- *Debt Ratio* shows if your business has enough assets to cover your debts.

  Debt Ratio = Total Liabilities ÷ Total Assets

Reminder...
Once you have gotten your Business Model, Marketing Plan, and Financial Plan in place, you can now take these very essential blueprints which have been used by many successful business owners as a guide to grow a profitable business, and begin to put them into action.

YOUR BUSINESS PLAN

A business plan consists of a set of plans that details your strategy on how you are going to reach your business goals. It serves as a communication tool for both internal and external users of the business plan, and it discloses past history of your business which is reflected in the Financial Statements. We covered the essential documents for getting your business off to a good start, listed below is a listing of the documents that make up a business plan and a brief description of their purpose.

Executive Summary: This is an overview of your business plan. It provides a glimpse of the content included in the business plan. This is one of the first sections an investor or financial institution will review.

Company Description: Detail information about your business, the unique factors that will make it competitive and what markets your business will be in.

Market Analysis: This is where key data about your business will be listed, industry outlook, competitive advantages and disadvantages, how you plan to overcome those competitive challenges, pricing information, target customers demographics, etc.

Organization and Management: List here information about your business structure and its owners, your company management team and their experience.

Products or Services: What products you sell or the services you provide and the benefits to your customers.

Marketing and Sales: This is a summary of your marketing and sales strategy, detailing how you plan to acquire and retain your customers.

Funding Explanation: If you will need a loan or investor, this is where you will state why you need the funds, how much you need, how you plan to use the funds and your plan on paying the loan back or how investors will get their return on investment.

Financial Information: This is where your financial projections are listed, your financial statements and financial ratios.

Appendix: List all other information here, such as copies of your licenses and permits, Accountant, Attorney, Resume, etc.

PART THREE

POSITIONING YOURSELF FOR SUCCESS

LESSONS IN BUSINESS

4

YOUR CHOICE OF BUSINESS STRUCTURES

*"A successful man is one who can lay a firm foundation
with the bricks others have thrown at him."*

~ DAVID BRINKLEY

Every successful business owner understands the importance of having the right business structure. Your business structure will impact how your business is taxed, if your business will be taxed, and the tax consequences to you as the business owner, partner or shareholder. In addition to taxability, your business structure will also determine your level of exposure to liability, what options you have to pay yourself, and how your income is treated: passive income, earned income or portfolio income. In this section you will learn the four most common business structures and some alternative variations of these business structures. Also, you will learn how the choice of business structure impacts how you and your business are taxed.

Before you can choose a business structure you must first understand the nature of your business. For example, do you sell products, offer services or both? As your business grows will you have to bring in partners or hire staff? Do you transact business with other businesses, consumers or government and how? How do you get your income? Are you the founder or operating under the umbrella of another entity? You need to understand the flow of activities in your business and the big picture. If you are new to business you may not understand everything initially, and this is normal. However, as your understanding and knowledge of your business increases things will become clearer, but the more certain you are about how things work in your business and which direction you want to take your business the better you can plan. If you have an understanding of your business before you choose a business structure, you are more likely to choose the best structure.

SOLE PROPRIETORSHIP

A business with one owner that has not been incorporated is a sole proprietorship. In a sole proprietorship there is no difference between the business and its owner. In other words, the business is not treated as a separate organization from the business owner. This also means that there is no liability protection in a sole proprietorship. For example, if the business defaults on its bank loan payments, the business owner will be held personally liable and the assets of the business owner can be taken to satisfy the debts.

Tax Impact

For tax purposes a sole proprietorship's income is reported on the individual tax return of the business owner. The Internal Revenue Service requires the business income and expenses being reported to be listed on Schedule "C" of Form 1040, U.S. Individual Income Tax Return. If the business has a profit for the year, the business owner will be subject to both "Federal" and "Self- Employment" tax. Let's take a closer look at "Self- employment" tax.

According to the Internal Revenue Service, the self-employment tax is the social security and medicare tax, primarily for individuals who work for themselves. It is similar to the social security and medicare taxes withheld from the pay of most employees. If you were to be working as an employee of a company, your employer is normally responsible for paying the salaries and wages to the employees, and in the United States half of the 15.3 percent FICA taxes which consists of two parts: 12.4 percent for social security (old-age, survivors, and disability insurance) and 2.9 percent for Medicare (hospital insurance). The tax amounts are based on a predetermined percent as determined by government regulation. Employers must pay 1.45 percent of wages for Medicare taxes and 6.2 percent of wages for social security taxes up to the annual maximum and the other half is deducted from the employee's paycheck. If you are self-employed, you will have to cover the entire 15.3 percent of self-employment tax and file Schedule SE (Form 1040) if your net earnings from self-employment are $400 or more. As for state taxes, generally, sole proprietors are not required to file a separate state income tax return since they are not a separate entity from the business and not registered with the state of organization. Therefore, in states requiring residents to file state taxes, the sole proprietor will file the individual return for that state.

LLC

The three letters "LLC" stand for *Limited Liability Company*. A limited liability company is formed by filing articles of organization with the state where the business will be established. Unlike a sole proprietorship the LLC is a legal entity separate from its owners, normally called members. Generally, all members are limited partners for liability purposes. This means that their personal liability for the business debts is normally limited to the amount of their investment in the business—their ownership percentage in the business and personal assets are not at risk. However, as with most entities, the extent of liability protection depends on other facts and circumstances—there are times when a member maybe personally liable. An LLC can be owned by one person, this is known as a *Single Member* LLC. A single member LLC's entity status is usually disregarded and therefore it is treated as a sole proprietorship unless the owner elects to be treated as a corporation. If the LLC is jointly owned it will be treated as a partnership unless the joint owners elect to be treated as a corporation, and the partnership tax rules will be applicable to the organization. If the LLC is jointly owned, in most states the management of the LLC can be by its members or managers. Manager members are treated in a similar manner as a general partner of partnership in the operations of the business. If an LLC has several members, to encourage order in the organization, the members may want to consider having at least one manager (not a member) to run the business especially if there will be other investors joining the LLC in the future. If there are only two members, it may be more reasonable to have the member(s) manage the business. An LLC has both the characteristics of a corporation and a partnership, it offers its members protection similar to a corporation—but limited, and it is treated like a partnership. To elect the Corporate status, the individual or joint owners will file form 8832, *Entity Classification Election* with the Internal Revenue Service. Further, the owner(s) may also elect to be treated as an "S" corporation by filing form 2553, *Election by a Small Business Corporation* under section 1362 of the Internal Revenue Code. "S" *corporations are explained later in this section.*

Tax Impact

If an LLC has only one member, a single member LLC, then for tax purposes it will be treated in the same manner as a sole proprietorship. Business income and expenses will be reported on Schedule "C" of Form 1040, U.S. Individual Income Tax Return. If the business has a profit for the year, the business owner will be subject to both "Federal Income" tax and "Self-Employment" tax. If the LLC elected the corporate status then it will file as a corporation. If the LLC did not elect the corporate status and it has more than one owner it must file as a partnership. Businesses that may be suitable for LLCs are real estate investment entities, small consulting firms, marketing and other service based or retail operations seeking some form of liability protection with minimal requirements and flexibility to change the entity as the business grows.

PARTNERSHIP

There are two types of partnerships, General Partnership (GP) and Limited Partnership (LP). A General Partnership is not required to file a formal partnership agreement with the state in which it is organized in order to be a legal entity. To be recognized as a legal entity separate from its owners under state law, both partners may establish with a written agreement between the partners or join together in an activity to generate business profits. To form a Limited Partnerships, a certificate of limited partnership must be filed with the state where the partnership will operate. The key differences between a general partnership and limited partnership are that in a general partnership all partners are considered to participate in the day-to-day operations of the business as general partners normally do, and they are all liable for the debts of the business. Whereas, in a limited partnership, there must be at least one general partner who controls the day-to-day functions of the business and is responsible for the partnerships debts. All other partners do not actively participate in the management of the business, as such their personal liability is capped at their investment in the partnership, and their personal assets cannot be used to pay off business debt.

Tax Impact

A partnership does not pay tax; it only files an information tax return known as Form 1065, *US Return of Partnership Income*. It is the partners of the partnership that pay taxes, this is way a partnership is called a flow-through entity. In a flow-through entity, any business income or loss flows from the business to the owners, shareholders, or in the case of a partnership—the partners, according to their share of ownership through what is called a *Schedule K-1, Partner's Share of Income, Deductions, Credits, etc.,* and reported on their personal income tax return. Partners who are passive do not pay self- employment taxes while active partners do. Also, active partners receive Guaranteed Payments, which is a set amount of payments to the partners instead of salaries. Listed below is an example of what you could write for your guaranteed payment agreement.

John and Katherine will be guaranteed a payment, each year from the business, of forty percent of the profits, but not to exceed $50,000 each. This agreement would be signed by both partners and kept safe.

Sometimes in a partnership, the partners may choose to take a *Draw* instead of guaranteed payments as compensation and the tax effects of both are very different. A draw also known *as Distributive Share of Profits* will reduce the partner's basis. Basis is the amount of money, or value of property a partner contributed to the partnership to start it, and keep it going. Because a draw is treated by the Internal Revenue Service like a return of capital on the amounts that were invested into the business, it is not deductible for tax purposed by the business. Guaranteed payments are tax deductible by the business. Some self-employed people incorrectly think that their draws will be a deduction from the gross revenues of the business, but this has long been a misunderstanding that most people make. So in order for the draws to be counted as a reduction to the business it must be in the form of a guaranteed payment.

CORPORATION

Founders of a corporation must file articles of incorporation with the state where the company is organized in order to be recognized as a legal entity separate from its owners. Corporation owners are called stockholders or shareholders; this is because ownership interest in a corporation is obtained by acquiring shares of stock in the company. A corporation is the only entity that offers full liability protection for its shareholders, but it has more requirements that must be followed and its earnings are subject to double taxation. Double taxation takes place in a corporation when the profits of the corporation are taxed for federal tax purposes, and again when the corporation distributes dividends to the shareholders from profits that were already taxed— the shareholders are taxed on this distribution of dividends at their personal income tax level. A shareholder can become an employee of the entity and receive a reasonable salary for their services, an option not available in a partnership.

What's the difference between an LLC and a Corporation?

LLCs and Corporations both provide protection against personal assets being seized to cover business debts, but LLCs have limited protection and fewer requirements that must be followed. In spite of the double taxation, if you plan to have investors and public shareholder in the future, a corporation maybe more suitable since there is no limit on the number of shareholders that a corporation can have. Also, a corporation allows for more organization in the management of the company as supposed to an LLC which allows members to run the business. Issues may arise in the LLC if there are too many member managers trying to run the day-to-day operations of the business, or even with investor partners. This is not always the case, but it is usually good to consider all possibilities and choose the best structure for your business. Tax deductibility of certain fringe benefits and the salaries of shareholder-employee, including the ability to raise capital have made owning a corporation more attractive. For example, a corporation can offer an employee stock ownership options; this can be a competitive advantage in bringing on and retaining great talent in your growing business since LLC's do not issue stock. But in a partnership LLC, you can turn your valued employee into a partner by offering him/her a small ownership percentage in the business, for example a 5% ownership interest. Considering the complexity of the tax laws and its constant changing nature, it is advisable to speak with a tax accountant or attorney for further guidance on your specific scenario.

S Corporation

The "S" Corporation is a federal tax hybrid by design, similar to an LLC partnership with some benefits of a Corporation. It is legally formed by filing articles of incorporation with the state of organization in order to be recognized as a corporation, and filing *Form 2553,*

Election by a Small Business Corporation under section 1362 of the Internal Revenue Code, to elect the "S" corporation status. The "S" corporation looks like a partnership, but partnership rules do not apply in every aspect. An individual can own an S corporation, income or loss from the business passes to the shareholder, and the shareholders are protected from being held liable for the debts of the business as long as it's a domestic corporation. An "S" corporation files an information return named, Form 1120S, *U.S. Income Tax Return*, whereas a C corporation files, Form 1120, *U.S. Corporation Income Tax Return*.

In exchange for the single taxation level, S corporations are currently limited to 100 shareholders in the company; however husband and wife count as one shareholder. Annual meeting and minutes of the meeting are required as in a C corporation, and shareholders are not subject to self-employment tax on distributed earnings.

All forms of organization except the "C" corporation are flow-through entities; this is because all income or loss passes through to the business owners and reported on their personal tax return.

Tax Impact

A "C" corporation files and pays its own taxes because it is a completely separate entity from its shareholders. Another level of tax is paid by the shareholders when they receive their 1099-Div, *Dividends and Distributions* Form for income reporting. The tax rates for a "C" corporation are progressive, similar to that of an individual. Tax rates start at around fifteen percent and progress as profits from the business increase. The "S" corporation's income passes through to the shareholders and is taxed to the shareholders at their personal tax rate. Income from the "S" corporation is reported on schedule "E" *Supplemental Income and Loss* of Form 1040 and it is not subject to the self- employment tax.

Which business structure should you choose?

Tax laws are very complex, as such providing guidance on which business structure to choose without knowing all the essential data about a particular business and its owners is not advisable. The information contained in this chapter has been provided to bring awareness of the most common business structures in the United States. In addition, although this book shares the general tax consequences of selecting a particular business structure, there may be other issues that may impact your taxes, like contributing property to a business, owing multiple businesses, and partnership agreements. Therefore, every situation is unique and should be discussed with your tax accountant or tax attorney for guidance on your specific situation.

NOTES:

_____
_____
_____
_____
_____
_____
_____
_____
_____
_____
_____

LESSONS IN BUSINESS

The taxes discussed in chapter five pertain particularly to individuals who are self-employed in the United States. While most of the lessons in this book are applicable to any solopreneur building a business throughout the world; chapter five addresses individuals planning to operate or currently operating in the United States. Please consult with an accountant or tax expert in your country for relevant tax laws.

5

BUSINESS TAXES YOU SHOULD KNOW

"Every action needs to be prompted by a motive."

~ LEONARDO DA VINCI

Several business owners become overwhelmed when they realize how many tax situations they need to keep up with. Some business owners learn about the tax implication of various transactions as they arise. Unfortunately, countless businesses have gone into debt or closed because the business owners were unaware of their tax responsibilities. In this section you will learn about the general tax responsibilities of self-employed people. But first you need to get an idea of the purpose behind taxes, because it's not fair to pay so much money in taxes and you have no idea why you are paying it—well, at least the supposed purpose.

Why do we pay taxes?

Taxes influence the decisions of consumers and business owners every day, and it has been that way for centuries. But many people are afraid of taxes because they do not understand the purpose behind taxes, and for others the very idea of having their hard earned money taken from them and their families is frustrating. So, the desire to preserve earnings coupled with the lack of knowledge about taxes, and the distrust of what residents tax dollars are being used for, causes stress for so many people. Taxes in general, is the government's way of raising money to fund its projects for the benefit of the country. The Government has a budget for things that it wants to accomplish, and since it is supposed to be for the benefit of the citizens and residents of that country, everyone earning money is required to contribute to the country's fund. Now, in the U.S. we are supposed to have a fair tax system which requires the tax burden to be assigned to each person and business according to their ability to pay. But our tax system is progressive, this means that the more earnings you have for the year, the more you shall pay—well, unless you know how to take advantage of the tax laws. Some see the progressive tax system as a *Robin Hood* situation, where money is taken from the rich (those who earn more) and given to the poor (those who earn very little or nothing at all) simply because they have more. But most of the wealthy people today started with very little and worked their way up the ladder (self- made)—sort of like what you are doing with your business. No one likes their property taken from them unwillingly, as such many others believe that a fair tax system is one in which everyone pays the same tax; perhaps ten to fifteen percent of their earnings—a *flat tax*.

Federal government taxes pay for our national security, military and other government workers salaries, programs that benefit the poor and those with special needs, etc., we will go over state taxes later. There are some programs that have been established and not properly monitored, and this is when people get upset; especially when there always seems to be a deficit problem. Some people over the years have tried to take government tax matters into their own hands, by limiting their income potential, so they don't have to pay taxes—not recommended. Why live a lesser quality life because of taxes, don't let it control you, but rather exercise power by knowing the taxes that affect you, and plan ahead so that you can use the tax laws properly to reduce your tax liability and increase your after tax money. The people who always seem to pay the least possible taxes are the ones who are savvy with the tax law, have a really good tax accountant, or a tax attorney. Many times, when the government really wants to push an initiative they will give a tax credit or offer a tax deduction to either reward people for helping out, or give them an incentive to act. For example to encourage more people to get an education, the government gives an education credit, to encourage donations to charities, there is a charitable deduction, and to promote energy conservation, the government offered the federal tax credits for energy efficiency. Taxes are only imposed by the government: federal, state, or local, so always make sure that a tax bill is from a government entity. Discussions on tax issues could go on forever, but it's more important for you to understand what taxes apply to you. Let's start by first revisiting the self-employment tax that was mentioned in chapter four.

SELF-EMPLOYMENT TAX

Self-employment tax is currently 15.3 percent of net profits. The tax is comprised of the Social Security and Medicare tax. The social security tax covers the monthly social security benefits for the retired, disabled and survivor individuals who qualify through the (OASDI),

Old-Age, Survivors, and Disability Insurance (OASDI) federal program. While the medicare tax pays for the medical insurance of individuals who are elderly or disabled. Social Security is funded through Federal Insurance Contributions Act tax (FICA). There is an annual limit for the amount of social security tax paid, the limits can be found on the U.S. social security website which is www.ssa.gov. There is no limit on the amount of medicare taxes paid. Self-employed business owners get an implicit deduction for the 7.65 percent employer portion of their taxes, 6.2 percent Social Security tax and 1.45 percent medicare tax. The 7.65 percent deduction results in what is known as net earnings being taxed, what this means is that only 92.35 percent of business profits are taxed. Further, once the tax has been determined, a deduction for 50 percent of the self-employment tax is allowed, resulting in you having to pay only one half of self-employment tax. You must pay self- employment tax and file Schedule SE (Form 1040) if your net earnings from self-employment were $400 or more.

QUARTERLY ESTIMATED TAX

It is important to note that if you owed tax during previous tax year or think you will owe a tax in the current year you are required to send in to the Internal Revenue Service quarterly estimated taxes. Table 5.1shows the IRS general rule for estimated tax payments. If you are not sure, you may want to send it in any way to ensure that you are in compliance with regulation. Quarterly Estimated tax is the method used to pay your Social Security, Medicare and Income tax. Once you become self-employed you no longer have an employer withholding these taxes for you, therefore sending in a quarterly estimate will lessen the burden of sending in a lump sum tax payment when taxes are due. The tax worksheet in Form 1040-ES, Estimated Tax for Individuals, is used to figure these taxes. You will need your prior year's annual tax return in order to fill out Form

1040-ES, so be sure to keep all tax workpapers organized in a file (electronic or physical folder).

Table 5.1 IRS general rule about estimated taxes

General Rule

In most cases, you must pay estimated tax if both of the following apply.

1.   You expect to owe at least $1,000 in tax for upcoming tax filing year, after subtracting your withholding and refundable credits.

2.   You expect your withholding and refundable credits to be less than the smaller of:

> a) 90% of the tax to be shown on your upcoming (current) tax filing year.

> b) 100% of the tax shown on your prior year tax return.

> c) Your tax return must cover all 12 months.

*Your estimated tax is based on **total tax** not the amount you sent to the Internal Revenue to cover the difference in the prior year amount owed.*

Exception

You do not have to pay estimated tax if you were a U.S. citizen or resident alien for all of the tax filing year and you had no tax liability for the full 12 month tax filing year. You had no tax liability for the tax filing year if your total tax was zero or you did not have to file an income tax return.

There are special rules for higher income taxpayers based on your adjusted gross income (AGI) for the tax filing year. Substitute 110% for 100% under General Rule. See Internal Revenue Service Publication 505 for AGI requirements.

CALCULATE YOUR QUARTERLY ESTIMATED TAX

Start with your previous year tax return and take a look to see what your total tax was, you may have to use this figure to determine your quarterly payment.

1. Determine your expected adjusted gross income, taxable income, taxes, deductions, and credits for the year. Use your prior year's federal tax return as a guide to help you come up with a reasonable estimate. You can use the worksheet in Form 1040-ES to figure your estimated tax also.

2. Once you have determined your expected gross income for the current year, use the current year's *Tax Rate Schedules* to determine your tax. Tax rate schedules can be found in Publication 505, Tax Withholding and Estimated Tax.

3. After estimating your upcoming year's tax, check the general rule and choose the best option.

4. Divide your tax into four equal installments and pay each one by the due date.

PAYMENT DUE DATES

Your estimated tax is due by the dates shown below.

- 1st payment .April 15
- 2nd payment . . . . June 15
- 3rd payment . . . . Sept. 15
- 4th payment .Jan. 15

MAKING YOUR PAYMENT

Form 1040-ES also contains blank vouchers you can use when you mail your estimated tax payments, or you may make your payments using the Electronic Federal Tax Payment System (EFTPS). If this is your first year being self-employed, you will need to estimate the amount of income you expect to earn for the year. Remember, you do not have to pay estimated tax for the current year if you **meet all three** of the following conditions: (a) you had no tax liability for the prior year, (b)you were a U.S. citizen or resident for the whole year, and (c)your prior tax year covered a 12 month period. *You had no tax liability for the prior year if your total tax was zero or you did not have to file an income tax return.*

If you estimated your earnings too high, complete another Form 1040-ES worksheet to refigure your estimated tax for the next quarter. If you estimated your earnings too low, again, complete another Form 1040-ES worksheet to recalculate your estimated taxes for the next quarter. You can use these estimated tax payments to pay your self- employment tax in advance. If you overpay on your estimated tax, you may choose to have the excess refunded or applied to your next year's estimated tax payment. If you do not send in the minimum estimated payment, you may be subject to the Underpayment Penalty. If figuring out your estimated tax seems complicated, get a tax accountant to calculate it for you, and you can simply make the payments electronically or by mail.

EMPLOYMENT TAX

If you choose to hire employees to help you in your business, there are a few tax compliance requirements you need to be aware of. To avoid errors in reporting you may want to consider outsourcing your payroll administration and employee management to a payroll solutions company. The internal revenue service requires that all employers withhold federal income tax from employees' wages. To figure out how much tax to withhold, use the employee's Form W-4 and withholding tables described in IRS Publication 15,

Employer's Tax Guide. You must also withhold part of social security and medicare taxes from your employees' wages. This is half of the 15.3 percent FICA tax or 7.65 percent, of which 6.2 percent is allocated to Social Security tax and 1.45 percent medicare tax, and you must match the other half.

Each quarter, all employers who pay wages subject to income tax withholding (including withholding on sick pay and supplemental unemployment benefits) or social security and medicare taxes must file Form 941, Employer's Quarterly Federal Tax Return. Form 941 is used to report the withheld taxes, and it must be filed by the last day of the month that follows the end of the quarter. Withholdings must be deposited by electronic fund transfers using the IRS's Electronic Federal Tax Payment System (EFTPS). You must also report and pay FUTA (Federal Unemployment Tax Act) tax separately from Federal Income tax, and social security and Medicare taxes. You pay FUTA tax only from the business funds. Employees do not pay this tax or have it withheld from their pay.

UNEMPLOYMENT TAX

If you hire an employee to help you in your business you may be required to pay unemployment tax. The unemployment tax goes towards funding the temporary unemployment benefits for individuals fired from their jobs without reason. One way to avoid having to pay unnecessary payroll taxes is to determine if you need someone on staff full-time or part- time—higher payroll means higher payroll taxes, and whether a contractor will meet your needs instead of an employee. Listed below is the Internal Revenue Service view on Employee vs. Independent Contractor.

1. The general rule is that an individual is an independent contractor if the payer has the right to control or direct only the result of the work and not what will be done and how it will be done. The earnings of a person who is working as an independent contractor are subject to Self-Employment Tax.

2. You are not an independent contractor if you perform services that can be controlled by an employer (what will be done and how it will be done). This applies even if you are given freedom of action. What matters is that the employer has the legal right to control the details of how the services are performed.

3. Under common-law rules, anyone who performs services for you is your employee if you can control what will be done and how it will be done. This is so even when you give the employee freedom of action. What matters is that you have the right to control the details of how the services are performed. You can review this information on the IRS's website. Further, if you employ the services of an independent contractor, you are required to keep a W-9 on file for each contractor. A W-9 certifies the tax id or social security number of the person you are contracting. It is also part of your backup support in the case of an audit, as proof that you are not falsifying deductions for payments made to contract laborers. You can obtain a W-9 form from the IRS's website.

STATE TAX

One of the ways that states generate revenue is through taxes. State income from taxes go towards funding programs that pay for schools, fire and police departments, transportation and various other needs. Businesses may be required to pay income tax to the state where they are headquartered. Each state has their own state tax rules for businesses and individuals, as such it is best to consult with a tax consultant or tax attorney about your specific state's tax compliance requirements. If you derive business income from other states, you may be required to file and pay tax in each of those states as well as to the state where your business is headquartered. Some state taxes that a business owner may be responsible for are sales tax, use tax, property tax, and income tax.

SALES TAX

Retail businesses are required to collect sales tax from its customers and remit those sales taxes to the states where they are conducting business. A retailer's responsibility is simply to collect the tax on the items they sold to their customers and send the taxes collected from the sale of goods to the state, generally on a monthly basis unless other arrangements were made with the state. To determine if you are required to file and pay tax in another state, there must be a business connection or physical presence in that state, this is known as *Nexus*. Nexus is created in a state if you have sales representative, independent contractors, employees or property, such as an office, delivery truck, or inventory in a state. State tax rules are different in each state, and sometimes determining if you truly have nexus can be a little unclear, so consult with your tax accountant or attorney for clarification. The information provided in this book is to bring awareness to you so that you can plan ahead for success.

USE TAX

Use tax is a tax on goods and services (see your state's tax rules on this) purchased by a business or an individual outside of their state. Since the goods were not purchased in the state no sales tax was collected, so when goods are purchased outside the state and brought in for use by the business, a use tax is assessed. In general, if a sales tax would have been assessed on it, then a use tax may likely be applicable. Your state may also allow a credit for sales and use tax paid to another state on the property or services brought into the state. A tax is usually assessed on taxable property or services purchased outside your state, made over the internet, by phone or catalog, purchased on an Indian reservation, property with a resell certificate, or property used that was purchased with an exemption certificate, these are just a few examples. For more information on use tax, visit your state sales and use tax office or website.

PROPERTY TAX

Many business owners are unaware of their responsibility to pay business property tax until the taxing authorities show up for an audit at their place of business. Sometimes referred to as *Business Personal Property Tax*, is a tax levied by the local county taxing authority on business assets, such as equipment, furniture and fixtures, inventory held for sale, computers and in some cases work-in- process if you manufacture your goods for sale on location. Simply put, any business property used in the operations of the business to generate income could be subject to property tax. Business are required to submit on an annual basis, a form listing each business asset, its location, the description of the asset, the cost and the date of purchase , to the local appraisal district. The list is then reviewed by the appraisal district to determine the current market value on the property before a tax rate is applied to obtain the property tax due to the local taxing authority. The tax assessed is usually on the business property market value. In many cases business property that is leased by the business must also be included on the appraisal form with a note explaining the circumstances. Leased property indicated on the form will be used to locate and assess the actual business owner for the property. If instructions for reporting leased property are not followed properly, you could be assessed with the tax responsibility. Home based businesses with business equipment are also required to pay business personal property tax. Keep in mind, the reporting is for property owned by the business, and used in the operations to generate income. Speak with your local tax assessor's office for further details.

TAX PROJECTIONS

A tax projection is one of the planning tools used by successful self- employed business owners to avoid surprises at tax time, and to maintain control over their finances. Tax projections help you determine if you will owe a tax in the upcoming tax year, how much you may owe, if will you get a refund and how much. It can also expose areas of opportunity for tax planning, which will allow you to implement tax strategies to lower your tax bill and maximize after tax profits. The best time to run a tax projection is towards the end of the year when you have a clearer understanding of what your income is likely to be, usually in the fourth quarter of the year.

You may purchase software to run your own tax projection or have your accountant to do it for you. Here are a few items that you will need to have in order to run a proper tax projection; (a) your bookkeeping will need to be up to date, (b) you will need your prior year's business and personal (federal and state) tax returns so you can identify amounts from the prior year that will be similar for the current year, and to identify the previous year disallowed credits (carryovers) to be included in the upcoming tax year filing, and (c) your current year-to-date profit and loss statement. Take your total year-to-date gross income and divide it by the total months past for the year (you may include the current month). This will show your average monthly income—multiply this figure by twelve. This is your *estimated* gross income for the year, this is known as *income annualizing*. Include any other income items that you expect to receive and deduct all your expenses you anticipate for the year. Use the tax tables in the IRS 1040 instructions booklet to determine your estimated tax. An example of using a tax projection to your advantage would be to determine, once you have an idea of what your tax may be for the upcoming tax year, whether to purchase equipment in the current year that you were planning to buy and take the depreciation deduction now or hold off until the next year and take the deduction at that time.

Year-End Tax Checklist

Have these items ready for your accountant at tax time, all items may not apply to you.

- Bank statements for the year.
- Credit card statements for the year.
- Business checkbook.
- Cash receipts (if applicable).
- **Payroll detail:** *Contract labor pay record (W-9), Form 940 employer's annual federal unemployment tax return (FUTA),*Form 941*employer's quarterly federal tax return,W-3 wage and tax statements* from paying employees, this is the sum of all the W-2s.
- Your final year reconciled bank statement (December 31st).
- Forms 1099-MISC, Forms 1099-K, Form 1099-Int, Form 1099- Div.
- Copy of your prior year tax return (federal and state).
- List of business fixed assets, furniture, fixtures and equipment.
- **Home Office:** *Square footage of home, Square footage of office space, office equipment purchased for the year, utilities, mortgage statement, rent, receipts for up-keep of home.*
- **Inventory schedule:** *beginning balance, total purchases for the year, and ending balance.*

NOTES:

_____
_____
_____
_____
_____
_____
_____
_____

Tax and Credits	38	Amount from line 37 (adjusted gross income)		38
	39a	Check if: ☐ You were born before January 2, 1949, ☐ Blind. ☐ Spouse was born before January 2, 1949, ☐ Blind. } Total boxes checked ► 39a ☐		
Standard Deduction for—	b	If your spouse itemizes on a separate return or you were a dual-status alien, check here ► 39b ☐		
• People who check any box on line 39a or 39b or who can be claimed as a dependent, see instructions.	40	**Itemized deductions** (from Schedule A) or your **standard deduction** (see left margin) . .		40
	41	Subtract line 40 from line 38		41
	42	**Exemptions.** If line 38 is $150,000 or less, multiply $3,900 by the number on line 6d. Otherwise, see instructions		42
	43	**Taxable income.** Subtract line 42 from line 41. If line 42 is more than line 41, enter -0- . .		43
• All others:	44	**Tax** (see instructions). Check if any from: **a** ☐ Form(s) 8814 **b** ☐ Form 4972 **c** ☐		44
Single or Married filing separately, $6,100	45	**Alternative minimum tax** (see instructions). Attach Form 6251		45
Married filing jointly or Qualifying widow(er), $12,200	46	Add lines 44 and 45 . . . . ►		46
	47	Foreign tax credit. Attach Form 1116 if required	47	
	48	Credit for child and dependent care expenses. Attach Form 2441	48	
Head of household, $8,950	49	Education credits from Form 8863, line 19	49	
	50	Retirement savings contributions credit. Attach Form 8880	50	
	51	Child tax credit. Attach Schedule 8812, if required . . .	51	
	52	Residential energy credits. Attach Form 5695	52	
	53	Other credits from Form: **a** ☐ 3800 **b** ☐ 8801 **c** ☐	53	
	54	Add lines 47 through 53. These are your **total credits**		54
	55	Subtract line 54 from line 46. If line 54 is more than line 46, enter -0- . . . . ►		55
Other Taxes	56	Self-employment tax. Attach Schedule SE		56
	57	Unreported social security and Medicare tax from Form: **a** ☐ 4137 **b** ☐ 8919		57
	58	Additional tax on IRAs, other qualified retirement plans, etc. Attach Form 5329 if required . .		58
	59a	Household employment taxes from Schedule H		59a
	b	First-time homebuyer credit repayment. Attach Form 5405 if required		59b
	60	Taxes from: **a** ☐ Form 8959 **b** ☐ Form 8960 **c** ☐ Instructions; enter code(s)		60
	61	Add lines 55 through 60. This is your **total tax** . . . . ►		61
Payments	62	Federal income tax withheld from Forms W-2 and 1099 . .	62	
	63	2013 estimated tax payments and amount applied from 2012 return	63	
If you have a qualifying child, attach Schedule EIC.	64a	**Earned income credit (EIC)**	64a	
	b	Nontaxable combat pay election **64b**		
	65	Additional child tax credit. Attach Schedule 8812	65	
	66	American opportunity credit from Form 8863, line 8 . . .	66	
	67	Reserved	67	
	68	Amount paid with request for extension to file	68	
	69	Excess social security and tier 1 RRTA tax withheld . . .	69	
	70	Credit for federal tax on fuels. Attach Form 4136	70	
	71	Credits from Form: **a** ☐ 2439 **b** ☐ Reserved **c** ☐ 8885 **d** ☐	71	
	72	Add lines 62, 63, 64a, and 65 through 71. These are your **total payments** . . . . ►		72
Refund	73	If line 72 is more than line 61, subtract line 61 from line 72. This is the amount you **overpaid**		73
	74a	Amount of line 73 you want **refunded to you.** If Form 8888 is attached, check here . ► ☐		74a
Direct deposit? See instructions.	► b	Routing number _____ ► c Type: ☐ Checking ☐ Savings		
	► d	Account number _____		
	75	Amount of line 73 you want applied to your 2014 estimated tax ► 75		
Amount You Owe	76	**Amount you owe.** Subtract line 72 from line 61. For details on how to pay, see instructions ►		76
	77	Estimated tax penalty (see instructions) 77		
Third Party Designee		Do you want to allow another person to discuss this return with the IRS (see instructions)? ☐ **Yes. Complete below.** ☐ No		
		Designee's name ► _____ Phone no. ► _____ Personal identification number (PIN) ► ☐☐☐☐☐		
Sign Here Joint return? See instructions. Keep a copy for your records.		Under penalties of perjury, I declare that I have examined this return and accompanying schedules and statements, and to the best of my knowledge and belief, they are true, correct, and complete. Declaration of preparer (other than taxpayer) is based on all information of which preparer has any knowledge.		
		Your signature _____ Date _____ Your occupation _____ Daytime phone number _____		
		Spouse's signature. If a joint return, both must sign. _____ Date _____ Spouse's occupation _____ If the IRS sent you an Identity Protection PIN, enter it here (see inst.) ☐☐☐☐☐☐		
Paid Preparer Use Only		Print/Type preparer's name _____ Preparer's signature _____ Date _____ Check ☐ if self-employed _____ PTIN _____		
		Firm's name ► _____ Firm's EIN ► _____		
		Firm's address ► _____ Phone no. _____		

Form **1040** (2013)

Figure 5.1 IRS Form 1040, line 44 is your actual tax, and this is the figure that your quarterly estimated tax payments are based on.

LESSONS IN BUSINESS

6

BUSINESS ESSENTIALS FOR SUCCESS

---

*"It is not good to have zeal without knowledge,
nor be hasty and miss the way."*

~ A PROVERB OF SOLOMON

Profitability! It matters in business, but equally important is making sure that all the essentials needed to get your business off to a good start have been secured. Covered in this section are easily overlooked fundamentals that help you have an efficient business. In section four you learned about business structures and their tax impact. However, in addition to liability protection offered by certain business structures, there are other benefits and essentials that you should know about also. For example, if you choose a business structure that requires you to register it with the state, the very act of registering your business protects your business name. Generally, if you operate as a sole proprietorship your business is not legally recognized as a separate legal entity.

Even though it's recognized in your local government, you have a tax id, and file your taxes annually; it's not recognized by the state as a legal separate entity. As such your business name could be snatched up and registered by another entity, but if you register your business with the state of organization, your business name will be off limits in that state. There are further steps you can take to protect your brand and company name on a national level, a business attorney can offer you guidance and solutions as your business grows. As you begin to realize growth in your business keep in mind the benefits of registering your business name and the legal protection it offers.

EMPLOYER IDENTIFICATION NUMBER

More and more self-employed business owners are realizing the importance of obtaining an Employer Identification Number (EIN). As noted by the IRS, an Employer Identification Number is also known as a Federal Tax Identification Number, and is used to identify a business entity. Many business owners get a federal tax identification number (tax id) for identity theft protection, and to keep business transaction separate from personal activities. For example, a retail business owner may buy merchandise at wholesale prices from a company where they have a membership. The wholesale company may require each business to have a tax id on file for identification purposes and other legal reasons. If the business owner uses the tax id for all business transactions it would offer more piece of mind than using their social security number. Also, when opening a bank account, the bank generally requires a tax id in order to create an account under the business name. In addition, when setting up electronic payment solutions, the merchant processing company is require to obtain a tax id to set up your business account and track revenues allocated to your business for 1099-K reporting which is required by the IRS.

BUSINESS BANK ACCOUNT

As customers pay you for your services and products, your funds should be deposited into your business bank account. Also, payments you make for business expenses should be deducted from your business account as well. Opening a business bank account will allow business transactions to be tracked separately from personal transactions, this becomes particularly important during an IRS audit. When business expenses are from a personal account, it may create doubt in the mind of the IRS agent. Further, if substantial evidence cannot be provided, the business expenses may be disallowed as a tax deduction by the IRS.

LICENSES AND PERMITS

A license is any form of authorization required by a regulatory entity in order to operate in a specific area or industry. Generally, a license offers the right to perform in a certain industry or profession for an undisclosed period of time as long as certain requirements are met. Other types of licensing are permits and registrations. Permits are usually issued by the local government in which the business intends to operate in (e.g. city or county). It gives permission to the business owner, authorizing him/her to conduct business in that particular locality. Most permits are temporary; this is what distinguishes it from a regular license. For example, a cosmetologist may be licensed to perform work as a hairstylist, but to set up shop and operate a hair salon in town the cosmetologist will need a permit from the city. In order to create clear ownership, state and local governments will sometimes encourage businesses to be registered.

One example of business registration is the DBA, which stands for Doing Business As, and commonly called Fictitious Name, Assumed Name, or Trade Name. Since Sole proprietors are not legal entities separate from their owners, one way they can show independent status is by getting an assumed name. An assumed name also allows business owners to show legal ownership of their business. When you register your business in the locality where you will be operating, it will be considered a legal business in that city. However, your business will only be separate in name but not from liability, because sole proprietors are still liable for all debts of the business. To maintain the right to operate in a city, many local authorities require annual renewal of permits. Permits are renewed by paying a fee, and depending on the industry business owners may be require to obtain certifications as well. To find out what license you need to operate check with your city government or industry regulatory at the state or federal level. Business owners operating without a license can be fined, closed down or even prosecuted.

BUSINESS LOCATION

COMMERCIAL LEASE

When deciding on a good business location most people think of easy access to customers and major roadways. This is because a business situated where there is a lot of foot traffic is likely to get more customers, but this is not the only factor to consider when deciding on a business location. Affordability, nature of business, and access to suppliers and vendors should also be considered. The thought of getting an office space may seem like a really good idea initially, but it may not necessarily be affordable at the moment. If you do need to get an office or retail space getting exactly what you want may not be the best course of action initially also. You should consider what your needs are, and if you have limited funds—it's affordability first, not primarily what you want. This is very important because under-capitalization is one of the main reasons people lose their business. If you choose to lease space, your rent payment is an overhead expense, and it should be factored into your business budgeted. In addition, utilities, phone, supplies, annual permits and maintenance cost will all be additional recurring expenses that you will incur and should budget for.

In general, there are 3 basic types of commercial leases, (a) the Gross Lease, (b) the Net Lease, and (c) the Modified Gross Lease. With the *Gross Lease* you will pay the landlord an agreed upon fixed amount every month for the space that you are using, and from that amount the landlord will pay the utilities, property taxes, insurance and maintenance. The Gross Lease is considered to be more tenant-friendly since the tenant pays a fixed amount and the landlord is responsible for paying all the expense regardless of the increase. *Net Lease* is the most common for retail establishments, it usually requires the tenant to pay a significant share of the cost associated with the property, so the base rents under the Net Lease is often lower or appears to be lower. There are several types of net leases but the most popular of them is the Triple Net Lease. The triple net lease is structured with the tenant's base rent stated separate from the additional expense. These expenses are Property taxes, Insurance and CAM—which stands for Common Area Maintenance. The common area maintenance is the general exterior areas of the property and usually includes water, sewer, trash, basic landscape, sprinklers and parking up keep. Many times, any interior maintenance will be at the expense of the business owner. The Net lease is considered to be more Landlord-Friendly since the property expenses are passed on to the tenants.

Lastly, there's the *Modified Gross Lease* which is pretty much like a hybrid of the Gross Lease and the Net lease. This lease agreement offers more of a compromise, where the landlord and tenant split the maintenance and sometimes the utilities, while the tenant will pay for the property taxes and insurance in addition to their monthly rent. So, when you are looking at the true cost of a renting a commercial space you must include property taxes, insurance and maintenance cost. The base rent is a fixed cost, which means that it will remain the same for the duration of the operating year. Fixed cost is good because you can plan your profit margins better with fixed cost.

However, while the lower base rent might be attractive, the property taxes, insurance, and CAM is a variable cost, which means it may go up at any point in time—usually on an annual basis, but it can increase before the year is over. So, what you are looking at is really a hybrid of fixed and variable cost for your total cost of leasing sometimes. The reason for the increase is that property taxes are based on the assessed value of the building, so as the value goes up, so will the property taxes. Insurance and maintenance cost will increase based on current market pricing. For example, if the sanitation department increase their rates it will be passed on to the tenant. So make sure that you assess the total cost of leasing a commercial space carefully.

A word about Build-outs or *leasehold improvements* which is the term we use in the financial accounting world. Whatever improvements you make to the interior of your leased space or additions that is attached to the building itself (meaning that it's a structural component) will belong to the landlord once you leave. You will have to depreciate the cost of the improvement over a thirty-nine year period. For example, if you put in a wall in your space to create a seating area for clients or offices, you will depreciate it over a 39 year period; and when you leave that space it will go to the landlord. Sometimes business owners think that the landlord will give them a credit for the improvement or make a rent adjustment— sorry, that probably won't happen, if it was not negotiate before you signed the lease. Many times to make changes to your leased space you need the approval of the landlord to do so. Also before you sign any lease you should speak with your accountant about the possibility of amortizing your lease acquisition cost.

Repairs. You may be responsible for the repairs to your space or the building if it's a standalone building. Sometimes people notice that there's a leaking roof, and it will cost a lot to get it fixed—are you prepared to do that? Who picks the company to make the repairs? If you are responsible for the repairs you can perhaps choose according to your budget, but at times landlords want to ensure that the value of their property is protected and will want to approve who can do work on the property. This is even more so if it's major repairs where the physical structure of the property will be modified as supposed to basic repairs like faucets in the in the kitchen area or restrooms. Things can get very ugly, so make sure you ask the right questions or get an attorney to handle the lease for you. If the rent and related lease expenses are not paid timely, you maybe be locked out of your business, evicted and possibly lose everything or even sued. If payments are late, interest and penalties will also be incurred, which will increase the operating expenses and cut into business profits. While restaurants, manufactures, and retail stores absolutely need to lease space; service based businesses may benefit from a shared or virtual office lease program—let's look at these now.

VIRTUAL OFFICE

With a virtual office, for a minimal monthly payment you can get a small office to use for a certain number of times per month. Some packages include meeting rooms for appointments with clients, as well as mail and phone services. A virtual office is a nice option for self-employed people who work from home but need a professional setting to meet clients at. For example, an architect can do all the design work from a home office, when he/she has a meeting with clients or prospective clients, the virtual office and meeting room can be used. Having a home office is a great way to save money because there is usually no additional cost incurred from working from home. If there is a cost incurred, it is usually from redecorating the room to use as a designated office space, technology upgrades or a small increase to utilities. Whatever the decision, the cost must be considered and factored into the budget. Keep in mind that you may start off with one cost effective location and grow into a more preferred location as your business profits increase.

E-Business

The internet is also a location for a business. A business on the Internet is called an online business or e-business, which means electronic business. Both products and services can be offered in an e-business, some examples include retail stores selling their products online, membership services for access to exclusive travel deals, jobs, or movies; subscription services for access to magazines, tv shows, or videos, and so much more. The Internet is a business world all by itself with social networks, marketing options and the ability to expand a business reach with the integration of other digital platforms. For example, a business on the internet can be accessed on smartphones, making it easy for anyone to buy or sell from anywhere. An e- business may be a great starting place for many self-employed people because of the low start-up and maintenance cost. A retail business owner may want to harness the power of technology to grow their business before setting up a physical shop and incurring rental expenses.

With the advancement of technology, many businesses do not even have to keep inventory on hand. Manufactures and wholesaler are now providing a drop-shipping program in which a business owner can order products with their customized label and have it shipped directly to the customer. This is a very cost effective approach for self-employed retailers, because it reduces the overhead cost allowing more money to be allocated toward marketing or investing in other needed areas of the business. For a solopreneur who resides outside the city, an e-business will eliminate the concern for traffic and long commute time. However, business owners with a physical location will not only have to think about commute time, but also the business proximity to suppliers. Suppliers may charge for the delivery of inventory. If the business is located nearby, the business owners can pick up products easily or have them delivered conveniently for less. Construction is another factor, as ongoing construction for a developing neighborhood may discourage customers from visiting the business because of increased traffic.

Other things to think of before choosing a business location is how safe the neighborhood is, whether it fits with your brand, if the commercial space is move-in-ready, and if it needs renovations or a custom build out. Choose what fits best for your budget and works well with your business model.

BUSINESS INSURANCE

Choosing the right business insurance is sometimes confusing, but very necessary for self-employed business owners. Since sole proprietors are held personally liable for the debts of the business, having insurance can offer peace of mind and keep personal assets from being seized to cover debts. Listed below are some types of insurance available to business owners. An insurance agent can offer more insight on each of the options listed below.

Errors and Omission offers professional liability protection for mistakes and oversights on worked performed for clients. Errors and Omission is sometimes referred to as *Professional Liability Insurance*, and also *Malpractice Insurance* in the medical industry.

Property Insurance protects a business owner's assets, like office equipment, inventory, computers or building. If there was a theft, fire, or vandalism the insurance would cover these, as along as the insurance policy conditions are met.

General Liability Insurance provides damages if your products, services or even employees have been accused of causing bodily injury or property damage to a third party. Many insurance companies offer a general liability package bundled with property insurance, this package is called *Business owner's policy* (BOP).

Business Interruption Insurance protects your earnings if your business is not able to run due to a disaster. This policy is not usually sold alone, but as a supplement to a comprehensive policy or property insurance.

Commercial Auto Insurance covers vehicles owned by the business. If a business owner has vehicles used by employees of the business or used to transport goods, then this insurance will offer financial protection for damages to the vehicle caused by an accident.

Workers Compensation Insurance is required by most states if a business owner has employees. Workers compensation provides wage replacement to the employees who are injured on the job while working.

Data Breach Liability and Protection Insurance provides financial protection for the cost related to resolving the breach of client and employees sensitive information. For example, if a thief steals social security numbers, addresses and credit card information belonging to customers from the company database or files, then this insurance will offer financial protection associated with settling the issue.

Health Insurance is a major concern for many solopreneurs. In the United States, under the Affordable Care Act, you may apply for health coverage in the *marketplace*. Because you are a self-employed person you would apply as an "Individual", but you will first have to see if you qualify. To explore health insurance options under the affordable care act, visit www.healthcare.gov. If you or your spouse is considering making that big move to become a full-time business owner to focus on growing your business, you may want to consider taking what's known as COBRA, which means *Consolidated Omnibus Budget Reconciliation Act*. In the U.S. this is offered through your employer. It can buy you some time while you search for something more affordable as it is expensive, especially when looking at family rates. Under COBRA, you're entitled to continue purchasing health insurance from your former employer for up to 18 months. Just keep in mind that you may lose any contributions your employer made to the plan while you were an employee, and perhaps additional fees that your employer was responsible for. Now, if you absolutely cannot afford COBRA insurance, you do have the option of purchasing short-term or interim insurance to hold you over until you find the right policy for your budget and your medical needs. The short-term or interim insurance policies typically offer coverage for six months up to one year. You can also participate in a Health Savings Account (HSA), which requires you to make monetary contributions to pay for health cost. You may have to purchase a high deductible, low health premium, and stay healthy by exercising and eating right to keep your health cost down. A few great things about the health savings account include tax deductible contributions, the unused funds rollover form year to year, the interest earned on the HSA are not taxed and neither are your withdrawals taxed because you will be using them to pay for medical expenses. Some countries have a self- pay treatment or on demand health option, which may be a viable solution to ensure health coverage. For self-employed persons, money is what prevents many from having health insurance, so work your business to bring in the revenues and make the health insurance cost part of your budget.

OFFICE EQUIPMENT

In accounting, office equipment is categorized with the business' fixed assets. Most office equipment is used in the operations of the business to generate income or help make the process of doing business easier. Office equipment includes furniture and fixtures, computers, cash registers, fax machines, printers and copiers. So when choosing office equipment it should be relevant to the function of helping you to operate more efficiently so that you can enhance your customer's experience and generate income. Basic equipment like laptops and desktop computers should run fast and have certain business software installed like word processing, spreadsheets, antivirus, internet security, scheduling, accounting, web conferencing, data backup and storage, e-mail marketing and project management. While you may not need all of these it should get you thinking about what will make your business process better and save you time.

Furniture may not seem like much until it is viewed from the angle of brand marketing. If your products or services are great, but your office or store is a turnoff, prospective customers may assume that your work or the quality of your products are substandard. Further, business affiliates may not want to refer business your way because it may impact their brand indirectly as well. So, when selecting office furniture and décor make sure it aligns with your brand image or at least the message you want to convey through your design. Even if you are operating a home office, a nice interior design can inspire a positive work environment; it can give you a sense of accomplishment, and empower you to go further. Also, it can help you to feel good about yourself and your business. This can help you to convey a positive image, because when you feel good about yourself, you are more confident and it will show when you are speaking with clients in person or over the phone. Many times a nice interior design can be accomplished with a fresh coat of paint, a nice functional desk, a chair, some wall art, and plants.

BOOKKEEPING SYSTEM

What does the manila folder, the grocery store bag, the shoes box, the zipper bag and the legal size envelope have in common? Receipts! Most self-employed business owners use *cash basis accounting* which means that sales are recorded when the money is collected and expenses recorded when they are actually paid, so managing the books should be fairly simple. Tax time is usually when self-employed business owners get organized, but by then most of their receipts have faded, gone missing or they can't remember what it was for so they simply call it *miscellaneous*. The problem with this unofficial system is that your tax return is inaccurate and you end up paying more taxes than you should have to. In addition, by not organizing your books in a timely manner you lose the ability to monitor how efficiently you are managing the operations of your business. Successful self-employed people document every business transaction so that they will know how much revenue came into the business and how much they spent every month or even weekly. This process is known as: *keeping up the books*. The term books, in accounting refer to your profit and loss statement, your balance sheet and your cash flow statement.

When you are not actively monitoring your business transactions regularly, perhaps because you are so caught up in the daily acts of running your business, you eventually start managing your finances with a survival mentality. If you want to know where your money is going it is important that you review your books regularly. However, if you are really tight on funds monitoring should be done on a weekly basis or even daily to prevent surprises, and to keep you in control of your business finances. In addition, when you review your books frequently you are in a better position to plan and budget appropriately. This is because you will be able to see how much revenue dollars you brought in, what services or products it came from, how much you spent on specific operating and administrative cost—which will show you what product is selling and what costs have gone up. Once you know the answers to these questions, you can begin to analyze why it's working or not working and make the needed changes. For example, when planning your inventory purchases for the next month you can decide what needs to be replenished and how much of it is needed. You eliminate the necessity to guess, and make decisions on known facts; it is this knowledge that gives you the power to be in control of your business.

So what can I do to get organized right away?

To get organized right away, take all those loose receipts and put them into a spreadsheet. Shown in figure 6.1 is an example of a basic spreadsheet that could be put together by anyone with very little experience. Set up your spreadsheet by creating tabs for each month of the year. You can set up the first month and then once that month is over copy the template onto a new spreadsheet for the next month. Remove the prior month's numbers so that the template is blank and put the name of the current month on the spreadsheet as shown in the Figure 6-1, and remember to save your information. This method is a quick way to get organized if you are not able to afford an accountant yet. Some other cost effective options is to buy a bookkeeping software and install it on your computer or subscribe to a cloud-based accounting solution which is designed for small business owners.

You can buy bookkeeping software at an office supply store or order it online. Some of the software comes customized for the various industries, so most of the industry account listings (chart of accounts, see table 6.1) have been pre-titled making it convenient and easy to use. Cloud Base Accounting—bookkeeping management accessed from a remote server of a company providing you with computer storage, this allows you to access it from anywhere. You can take advantage of pricing that fits your budget, you can import expenses from your bank and credit card statements, integrate it with your online payment provider, some include the ability to create invoices and you can export the data to your accountant for tax preparation. You can access your accounting platform from anywhere and view your cash flow in real time. If you decide to manage your books in the cloud, once you register for a user account with your service provider you'll be up and running in very little time. The most important reason for being organized is awareness, staying informed so that you can maintain control of your business affairs. Take a look at figure 6.2, it shows one of the benefits you obtain from using an accounting software. It is a sample of a vertical analysis for a profit and loss statement. The analysis shows the percent of each expense based on sales revenue for twelve months; instead of creating it you select it and print.

Table 6.1 Basic chart of accounts examples

Assets	Liabilities	Equity
Checking Accounts Receivable	Bank Loan	Startup Capital Owners Draw

Revenue	Expenses
Sales Revenue Service Revenue	Supplies Salaries Contract Labor

Figure 6.1

Somewhere Company
Income and Expense Summary
For December 2014

Weeks	Revenue	Marketing	Office Expense	Meals	Auto Expense	Insurance	Professional Fees	Misellaneous
Week 1	$2,500.00	$ 150.00	$ 50.00	$100.00		$ 200.00	$ 100.00	$ 20.00
Week 2	$1,450.00	$ 200.00	$ 20.00	$150.00				$ 37.00
Week 3	$1,660.00	$ 350.00	$150.00	$100.00	$250.00			$ 10.00
Week 4	$1,690.00	$ 300.00	$300.00	$120.00				$ 25.00
	$7,300.00	$1,000.00	$520.00	$470.00	$250.00	$ 200.00	$ 100.00	$ 92.00

Total Revenue	$7,300.00
Total Expenses	$2,632.00
Total Profit	$4,668.00

Income and Expense by Month
January through December 2011

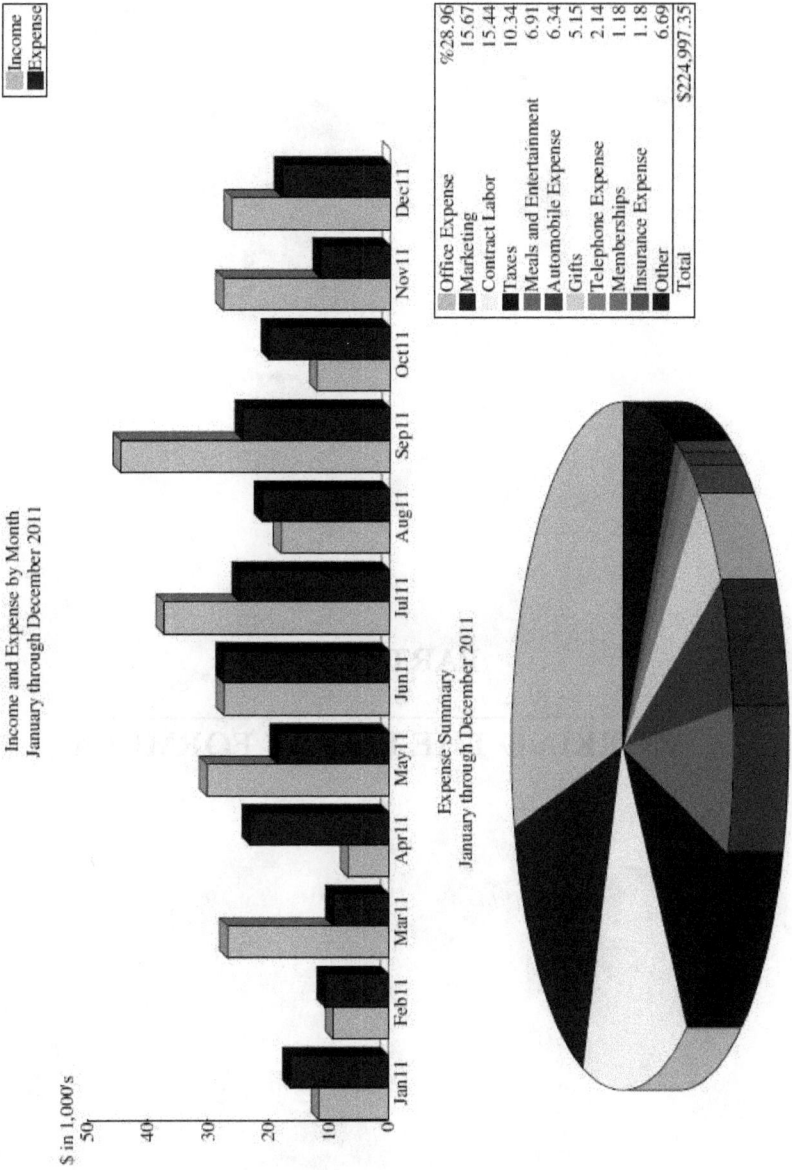

Expense Summary
January through December 2011

	%
Office Expense	28.96
Marketing	15.67
Contract Labor	15.44
Taxes	10.34
Meals and Entertainment	6.91
Automobile Expense	6.34
Gifts	5.15
Telephone Expense	2.14
Memberships	1.18
Insurance Expense	1.18
Other	6.69
Total	$224,997.35

Figure 6.2

PART FOUR

WORKING THE PROFIT FORMULA

LESSONS IN BUSINESS

7

GENERATING REVENUE

"Economic conditions are constantly changing, and each generation looks at its own problems in its own way."

~ ALFRED MARSHALL

What does having a thriving business mean to you? What does that look like? What can you change today in your business practice that could mean better earnings in the near future? How would that improve your life? At some point every business owner has thought about these question in some way. For many self-employed people it's generating more revenues. The struggle to generate revenues and the need to meet sales goals creates the desire to be better at bringing in customers. But many solopreneurs get stuck along the way trying to figure out what to do to get more customers. For several years business owners have searched high and low for the secret to generating more revenues. For those who got it, their *Aha moment* was realizing that it was in front of them all along—Marketing! How will anyone know that your business exist without you telling them? How will they know what you offer if you don't tell them? How will they know where to find you if you don't tell them? Actually, numerous businesses that were not profitable and eventually closed down, did so not because they mismanaged their money but because the business owner did not do enough marketing or the right kind of marketing. The reality is that many self-employed people know that marketing is very important for business growth, but their budget is not large enough to do the type of marketing that they think they need and really want to do. As a result they either do no marketing, or market on a tight budget, getting whatever they can afford hoping that something will work. It won't! Not without a strategic marketing plan.

In section three, you learned about Business Models, this is your starting point for coming up with a strategic marketing plan. With so many marketing options to choose from it can become very overwhelming just trying to decide where to allocate your money to get the best results. However, with a good business model in place you can have a better understanding of what you need to do to reach your target customers. Clarity! This is what your business model will help you to achieve, a clear direction about what you need to focus your marketing efforts on. Once you have gotten a clear understanding of who your customers are, what value you are offering them, and the channels you plan to use to deliver value to them, you can narrow your marking down to a few relevant choices and begin to test them out to see which one will provide the best results. By focusing your marketing efforts on what aligns with your business model, you can get greater returns on your investments. The choices you make will be well-thought-out and strategic, no blind guessing. Successful business owners do not guess, they are very purposeful and strategic. Even when using their instincts, successful business people align their strategy with their gut feeling in a tactful way. In this section you will learn the three active categories that every business owner must assess in order to determine where to focus their revenue generating activities. In addition, you will learn proven strategies that you can implement right away to help you improve your business growth. First, there are a few points that must be addressed. The first requires a trip to the world of Economics.

With so many ideas on how to get fast cash into your business, many business owners have gotten distracted and pulled away from the timeless principles of business. Have you ever wondered why there is so much information on how to generate revenue and make a profit; yet, several businesses are still failing and people are getting further into debt? Have you ever considered for a moment how people in emerging nations with tighter laws and far less resources are building profitable businesses? How can this be? Well, just as a house without a firm foundation cannot stand, so it is with business. There are principles that every small business owner should know, but unfortunately these principles are not usually taught. Such information is normally obtained if passed down from a parent with entrepreneurial experience, from a mentor who has business experience, by taking an entrepreneurial course, or expert advice provided on DVDs, CDs, or books like one you are reading now. Let's take a look at a few of these principles.

SUPPLY AND DEMAND

In microeconomics, which examines how people make decisions when the price of goods and services change, and its impact on the supply and demand of goods; emphasis is placed on British economist, Alfred Marshal's laws of economics. One of his laws states that when there is a demand for goods and supply increases, a surplus occurs, leading to a lower equilibrium price. Another way to see this principle is that when there is a demand for a product or service and there are many suppliers who offer this product or provide the service, the price of the product or service will decrease in order for business owners to maintain market share. This being the case, we can also say that when there is a demand for a product or service and there are few suppliers to offer the product or provide the service, the demand may drive prices up. To clarify both of these points, let's take a closer look. Let's say you are an insurance agent, and there are ten other insurance agents in your area, and there are several people who need insurance. These prospective customers can go to any of the ten agents to get what they need. All of the insurance agents will make a good living, but probably not that much difference from one another; making it a little more challenging to attain preferred revenue goals. If you want to direct more of the business your way and gain more market share you will have to set yourself apart by implementing a good marketing campaign and also offering quality services if you want to keep those customers. On the other hand, if you are one of the few offering a product or service that is in demand you can increase your prices and still maintain a good market share. For example, health care services provided by a doctor. If you are one of two doctors in town and you raise your prices people will still come because being healthy is of great importance and there are not many doctors offering this service. In this scenario, the doctor can perhaps do without much marketing because patients will spread the word about the great services and people are always looking for a good doctor. Sometimes an increase in price is used to attract serious clients who value your services. Now keeping in mind the first two principles, let's take a look at the flip side. If there is little or no demand (the demand went down) for a product or service and there are several people who offer this product or service, some of the business owners will likely go out of business because there's not much revenue coming in—sales are low. If one of the other business owners lowers his/her prices most of the customers will go to that business owner for services and as a result of the consumers behavior, all the other business owner may eventually go out of business. There are a few things that you should also understand with consumer behavior. If there is no need for a product, then a business owner will have a hard time making money and may eventually close the business and seek new opportunities. What happens with many self-employed business owners who find themselves in this position, is that they must now take on employment unwillingly to maintain their basic standard of living. But, if you diversify your sources of income by offering other services, going out of business may not be an issue.

You cannot force anyone to buy something they do not want. However, a great marketing expert knows how to create the need. So, if you have a really good product or service and there is no demand for that product or service yet, it could be that your consumers are not educated enough about the benefits. It is your responsibility to find a way to educate the consumers about the benefits of your product or service; this is one way you can overcome the lack of demand for a product or service. These are some of the most important principles in business that must be understood about consumer behavior, pricing and ultimately factors that may impact your business.

BRINGING IN THE MONEY

Now that you have an understanding of factors that can impact your business, let's take a look at the three active categories that you should assess in order to determine where to focus your revenue generating activities. Let's start the introduction of these categories with one of the questions that you must answer before you implement a marketing strategy: What do you want to achieve? In other words, when you say that you need to generate more revenue, what does that mean? What end result are you looking for? But you will also have to know *what specifically is missing*, so that you can address the issue and solve it with your marketing campaign. You should not start a marketing campaign without knowing the answers to these questions, because you must know why you are marketing, and to whom you are marketing. What do you need? When most self-employed business owners say they need to generate more revenue it is probably because they need, (a) more customers, (b) more channels of revenue, or (c) an image makeover.

The most common way self-employed people get customers is through word of mouth, which happens when you provide a service to an existing customer and they tell others about your services. The existing customer refers your services or products to their friends and family. This is the most powerful form of obtaining a client, because the referral is coming from someone that the prospect trusts. The opinion from the friend or family member is more valued, and most people share information about good things with people they care for and like. What you can do to encourage referrals is simply ask your existing customers to refer your services to their friends and family, you can enhance the chances of them doing so by offering a discount on their next purchase or establishing a *refer a friend* program with your business affiliates. If you do not have any business affiliates, you can join your local business chamber of commerce and other business networking organizations. Business networking organizations are a great way to meet prospective business affiliates; they give you the opportunity to get to know people through monthly meetings and events. By the time you have attended three or four events consecutively you will begin to get an idea of who you can start to build a business friendship with. These organizations are not free and some can be quit pricey, so manage your budget and expectations carefully. Some business owners join three or more organizations but realize that they cannot afford to attend all of them regularly, it is perfectly okay to join just one. Keep in mind that you are also self-employed so you need a realistic amount of time to allocate towards providing quality services for your customers and organizing your business affairs. In addition, when choosing a business organization, consider joining an organization that's not in your field of practice, this way you can meet people who may actually need your services. For example, if you are an attorney and you join your local business chamber in addition to the lawyers association. The chamber will increase your chances of getting more referrals and building new relationships, while the lawyers association is great for staying current of changes in the industry, best practices or taking continuing education courses. This strategy allows you to obtain the benefits that both types of business organizations have to offer.

For business owners who would like to join a business organization, but find it difficult because they have to be at their place of business most of the time, there are some organizations that do meet after business hours, lunch time or on weekends. Some business organizations offer training for their members, reduced price advertising in their publications and on their website. Some organizations even have a policy of only referring business to its members, that can be very powerful. Another point worth noting is that it takes two to build a business relationship, give and receive, so feel free to initiate the first call, e-mail or text message. Invite your new friend to lunch, get to know them and learn more about their services, and if you think that there is the slightest indication that you have something in common seize the opportunity. Everyone wants the same thing: to be successful in business.

Keep Working Your Business

While you wait for your customer referrals and business relationships to bloom, keep the momentum going by using social media to bring awareness to more people. Technology is not going away, it is actually advancing at a faster rate, so the sooner you learn how to use it to your advantage the sooner you can increase your revenue potential. From Facebook to Google advertising options, there are several internet-related services and products offering online advertising, and online social networking services to help businesses reach thousands of people daily. The key is to find what will work best for your business, the best fit to help you connect with your targeted customers. However, for self-employed people who may not be able to afford such a service at this time, The following are some things that you can do to get more customers.

Content Marketing

We live in an era of information and people want to know as much as they can before they commit to your product or service. Before consumers make a decision they need to feel like they can trust you. Content marketing is an excellent way to share your expertise or product information with prospective customers. It can help them understand what makes your product good or show them that you have a lot of knowledge in your industry. Content marketing is the creation of media or published articles to attract prospective clients to you. A few things you can do include placing short articles on your business website, in a magazine, or post a video to a social media site. If you chose to use content marketing to draw in more customers be sure to include your e-mail address or other information on how your prospects can reach you. In addition, you can also create a link for your website and e-mail address directly from the content.

Seminars and Workshops

You can host a workshop or short complimentary seminar for a product demonstration to show what you have to offer. It's like the chef who gives out food samples, or the trailers for a new movie, you want entice them and invite them to buy. If you choose to attract customers with a workshop or seminar, try having them when most people have some free time so that you can get more people to attend. For example, most people take a lunch break, and it's usually between half past eleven and two o'clock in the afternoon. So, you can schedule your event around lunch time and increase the chances of more people coming. But wait! These prospects are normally out for lunch at those times and they do want to eat, so what you can do to increase the likelihood of them attending your event is to offer them some lunch. This way they can save money by attending your lunch event, and you can get prospective customers who are alert and ready to listen. Lunch does not have to be extravagant, salad, finger food, and drinks at minimum will do. But you do need a place to host the event; you can use your office, rent a meet room in a hotel or a corporate space, team up with one of your business partners and have the meeting at their location, and in exchange for the favor, give them some platform time to talk about their business. Sometimes restaurants will even allow you to use their space for free as long as you are buying meals. Online seminars are also a great way to share your expertise with the use of virtual meeting room, web or video conferencing.

Video Conferencing: With video conferencing, people at two or more locations can communicate at the same time using two-way video and audio transmissions.

Web Conferencing: With web conferencing people can join a meeting from remote locations by logging into the hosting platform over the internet. Webinars, online workshops and interactive meetings are examples of web conferencing. Users can also do presentations and demonstrations without leaving their office or home. You can record meetings or presentations for others to access at a later date. Some require software or plugins before it can be used.

Virtual Meeting: This is an online meeting technology that allows people to meet with clients on the internet in real time using their personal computer. Aside from meetings, there's also video sharing and desktop sharing capabilities. No software needed.

E-mail Marketing

This form of reaching prospective customers has become more and more popular over the years. The reason many business owners enjoy using e-mail marketing is because prospects can subscribe to it by clicking the subscribe button to be included on the e-mail list and receive automatic e-mails from the business, it can also easily be forwarded to their friends, family and colleagues. In addition, business owners can modify designs to fit their brand and have a professional look. E-mail marketing is also a great way to build your database for future marketing campaigns. Common forms of e-mail marketing are newsletters, weekly updates, event invites, and promotional announcements. Listed in table 7.1 are some other wonderful ideas for you to get customers.

Table 7.1 Marketing Ideas

1. Post an Ad in your local newspaper (online or print version).
2. Sponsor an event for a local group, such as a charity, kid's school, a networking mixer, a local conference, trade shows or other event.
3. Join or attend a local meet-up group.
4. Advertise with the local business chambers.
5. Call your local radio station or television networks and ask about running a media ad campaign.
6. Market your services in a magazine.
7. Mail out postcards (they still work), check out the United States Postal Service, *Every Door Direct Mail®*, services for small business owners. You can send as much as you can to zip codes of your choice or based on your budget.
8. Advertise on your local paid access television stations.
9. Leave business cards or post cards at your business affiliates place of business (ask first).
10. Do joint marketing campaigns with non-competing businesses. For example a realtor and a mortgage banker can place both of their ads on a post card for bulk mailing or any print ads and split the cost of the campaign. Campaigns are advertisements that run for several weeks or months so that it is constantly in the face of prospects.
11. If your church has a business directory, list your business.
12. Post a *vlog* on a video sharing website; vlogs are video blogs but it can also be a web television. You can post a series of educational features, training sessions, or any other informational content.
13. Post a podcast. Typically podcast are short informational series in digital format and can be downloaded.
14. Post a picture of a banner or promotional ad on a photo sharing website.
15. Teach a community class and share your expertise.

CREATE MORE CHANNELS OF REVENUE

A common principle among savvy business owners is to diversify their sources of income. Most self-employed people have left their jobs as laborers for wages and salaries to explore the possibility of attaining financial independence through business ownership, and have never been taught to think like a business owner. Before their days as independent contractors, freelancers and sole proprietors, all that was known about diversification was in relation to retirement options like IRAs, 401(k)s, CDs, Stocks and Bonds. But diversification also has its place in business. Since nobody knows what the state of the economy will be in the near future or in the long run, every business owner should diversify their services or product offerings in order to have multiple streams of income. In addition, consumer behavior is subject to change and vendors or business partners may decide to discontinue their relationship with you in a moment's notice. So because you care about your financial wellbeing, it would be to your advantage to have multiple sources of income to help keep you out of a financial bind. There have been several self-employed people who have had the unfortunate experience of seeing a good paying contract cancelled. If you have multiple streams of income, you won't worry so much about it and can think rationally through the reorganization process because you are not solely dependent upon one contract, vendor, partner or product doing well.

Think Preservation

You do yourself a disservice when you only have one source of income when you are self-employed. Who's going to pay your bills when the money runs out or when your sales are slow? This does not mean that you should commit to products you don't believe in or provide services you don't like because you want additional streams of revenue. But you should take some time to assess what else you can offer. For example, if you are a singer, your albums should not be the only thing that you rely on. Perhaps you can write music, teach, establish retail merchandise, collaborate on other projects, setup your own internet channel with subscribers, or do live performances to reduce the risk of going broke.

This is even more of a requirement for self-employed business owners whose work is seasonal. If you are running a business that only brings in revenues during certain times of the year, then you have to figure out how you are going to bring in money during the slow months, if not you may find yourself in a real harsh financial crunch. You cannot assume that you will generate a lot of money from season to season because you cannot always predict what the economy will be like. Worrying about it will not solve it either, you have to come up with a strategic plan, and implement it so that you get through those months successfully. Even if you have consumable products you cannot assume that customers will be interested in that same product forever, nor can you assume that once you have a client that they will always use your services. Even though you may be able to forecast what sales maybe like during certain months, you should not leave yourself open for disappointment. You are a business owner, why put up with such inconsistencies? To avoid the headaches and worries, just diversify your income sources, but this is not all you must do. To keep more money in your bank account you must control your cost as well.

Put it into Practice

Let's take a look at some examples. Assume Sarah is a hairstylist specializing in hair care; she only services clients Tuesday thru Saturday. Sarah rents a small space costing her about $800 per month, a fixed cost. Sarah's only service is a package offer which includes shampoo, condition and style for only $75. Sarah currently sees about ten clients per week, that's $750 per week or $3,000 per month gross. Sarah rationalizes that she needs more revenue to truly make a profit after accounting for rent, supplies and other expenses. Well, instead of Sarah struggling to meet her financial obligation or worrying about how she is going to be profitable she revises her business model, financial plan, and marketing plan to accommodate a few suggestions she came up with for additional services. Sarah decides to offer deep conditioning treatments to existing clients for an extra $20 per client, and she picks up new clients through a new advertising campaign offering perms, relaxers, and color treatments averaging $250 additional income weekly. Sarah also added hair care classes every Monday evening for the general public which brings in another $175 weekly, and she also picked up a few more clients through the classes; that's an additional $2,500 added to her monthly income. Sarah now earns $5,500 every month, she can afford to hire part-time help to grow her business and take it to the next level. As Sarah's business continued to grow, she took some of the profits and bought some of her favorite hair care products at wholesale prices and sold them to customers at retail prices online and in the salon. Wow! Now that's being business minded. Let's look at one more example to help clarify the importance of diversification.

Miguel owns a men's boutique specializes in quality fine cotton shirts. He knows that it is usually a onetime purchase for many of his customers until the next seasons shirts are available for sale. So, in order to avoid low sales, which could cause him to default on his rent payment. Miguel had already determined as part of his plan to sell, men's khaki trousers, belts, ties and offer custom tailoring in his boutique. This way Miguel gets year round sales revenue. Miguel also writes a blog where he discusses the latest trends in men's fashion. This helps him to get new customers, and brings in additional revenue from the digital advertising space he sells to local complementary businesses, such as the sporting equipment shop and the men's barber shop. Miguel also hosts a men's wear fashion show once a year, a big event in which he donates 20% of the profits to his favorite charity. That's Business! That's Diversification! You will notice that in the two examples these business owners are offering complementary products and services. They specialize in one area that they do very well, but expanded within the same area of specialty. So do not overwhelm yourself by offering what you are not good at. Stay within your area of specialty—focus on growing in that area and you will excel at it.

Deepen Relationships

You now understand the importance of diversifying your revenue sources, but equally important is maintaining and nurturing the relationships you have with your existing customers. Get to know your customers a little more each time, so that you know what they like and how to package your offerings and present it to them. This is the easiest of all revenue generating strategies, you already have these customers, they are already doing business with you, why not suggest your other remarkable products and services to them. One reason that many self-employed business owners shy away from offering more to their customers is because in their own mind they feel like they would be pressuring their customers too much. But suggestions can be made in the form of a recommendation or friendly advice. In addition, the tone should not be forceful, but also friendly with a smile. Most consumers today are more educated and do notice the differences in tone and personality, they are also aware that they can spend their money on whatever they want. So approach your customers with confidence, care and kindness, because you only have them for that moment and you want them to come back.

Consider pairing services or products together and offering them at one price, this is known as bundling or packaging. For example, if you are an accountant, you can offer bookkeeping services, tax preparation, and a financial statement analysis for one fixed price slightly discounted. This is a great way to get more from a single sale deliberately. It is also saves your customers money, so in reality it is a win-win situation. You do not always have to discount the services or products, you can simple package it and sell it. Especially for products that should be used together in steps or services that are dependent on another service in order to be completed. For example, the accountant must first complete the bookkeeping in order to prepare the tax return, so it would make sense to offer this service as a package.

How to diversify your services or product offerings

Step 1
Take a moment to think about what else in your area of specialty you could offer to your customers. Write them down.

Step 2
Determine how much it will cost you to offer these products or services to your customers, and how much you are going to charge.

Step 3
Work them into your business model.

Step 4
Revise your financial projections to include your new products or services, and revise your budget to include the additional cost you will be incurring.

Step 5
Come up with a marketing campaign to let everyone know about what you have to offer.

GET AN IMAGE MAKEOVER

If there's one thing that should be common among businesses it ought to be Identity. Not that all businesses should be alike, but that they should all have their own identity. The distinctive quality that makes them stand out from the rest. People are unique, thumb prints are unique, and personalities are unique. It is the unique qualities in a person that people remember, and each business should have something special about it as well. If you are not converting prospects into customers and you have a good amount of exposure, then perhaps it could be that your prospects may not be sold on whatever it is that you offer. Perhaps you have too many product choices, perhaps you appear to be just like the rest.

Take a trip to the mall where some of the top stores are, try to see what makes these businesses unique. Take a look at the appearance of the stores, what message do you get in your mind about them? What story are they telling you? Take a look at their brochure, what is the message are they sending, upscale, trendy, traditional, urban down-to- earth, warm and cozy, cold and straight forward? How about well-known self-employed people, what message from their appearance do you get? As people, we naturally judge based on appearance before we even give anyone an opportunity. It's a natural radar that turns on in our mind as we try to determine a person's character in one look. As the saying goes "a first impression is a lasting impression", for many the first impression may be their only opportunity to make a lasting impression. This does not mean that you should ruin your budget to make a lasting first impression, but be the best you. If you can afford a fitted designer suit and not jeopardize your finances then go for it. If all you can afford is a $70 suit, then get the best your money can buy—shop around and get it. This is what you should also do for your business, because people judge based on the outward appearance and they only stay around if what was projected on the outside matches the character of the person, the work quality, or product quality. Likewise, if your business appears to be less than what your average target customers expect, they may not buy from you.

For example, if you are selling luxury homes this means you are catering to either the upper class consumers or the wealth class of consumers. No matter how good you are at what you do, if your first impression does not make them feel like they can trust you or that you can relate to them—it may be the last time you see them. So, you need to at minimum show up to the meeting looking like one of them. If you cannot afford a quality suit, then go elite business casual it will be much more appreciated and respected because image matters. It's not the most important thing, but it's been known to get many people in the door. While appearance may get your customers in the door, it's the quality of your products or service that will keep them coming back. Think of a store that you like, why do you like shopping there? What keeps you coming back?

If your marketing materials, website, office interior, and your appearance look tasteful then customers will assume that your products or services are quality. It sends the message that you care about your work. The focus is on your business image, brand, and output, not your personal life.

What is Branding?

Have you ever gone to buy a product and realized that you are buying the same product from the same manufacturer or retailer all the time? It actually takes a deliberate act sometimes to tell yourself to try another brand. But because you don't want to take chances and waist money, you just stick with what you already feel comfortable with. That's the impact a good brand will have in the marketplace. You may be wondering how you, as a self-employed person, can have that kind of impact. Well, it starts with the little things, like your logo and marketing materials–what message are they sending? Your business image and the experience your customers walk away with also matters. Even something as simple as how you do things in your business, including where you place your advertisements, and the colors you choose all say something about your business. Whatever experience your customers take away from doing business with you, it will always stick with them, and over time the loyalty grows as long as they continue to have that same experience. Branding can make a small company appear more established than it actually is. Your brand is how you or your business is perceived in the marketplace. Below are some solutions to help you build your brand.

Build Your Identity.
Rename your business, reinforce your brand with taglines and slogans and use them in all your marketing. If you don't have a logo get one, use your logo colors on all your marketing materials.

Stand-Out In The Crowd.
Breathe life into your exhibits, banners, posters, website, social media pages and other promotional products by redesigning them with eye catching designs and colors.

Simplify Your Product Line.
Streamline services or products to simplify what you offer so that it's clear to your customers. Using your profit and loss statement or your sales detail, take a look at what products or services are generating the most income and which ones are not. Then, using customer surveys find out why the best sellers are working and why the others are not. Phase out what is not working and restructure your marketing to promote these products in a new way. Your ability to adapt to change is important, so that you can maintain or grow your business.

TAX COMPLIANCE FOR REVENUE REPORTING

1099-Misc
The U.S. Internal Revenue Service requires trade or business payments to be reported on Form 1099-MISC for tax reporting by the recipient. Additional Internal Revenue Service requirements obtained from Form 1099-MISC instructions are listed below.

"File Form *1099-MISC* for each person to whom you have paid during the year: at least $10 in royalties or broker payments in lieu of dividends or tax-exempt interest; at least $600 in rents, services (including parts and materials), prizes and awards, other income payments, medical and health care payments, crop insurance proceeds, cash payments for fish (or other aquatic life) you purchase from anyone engaged in the trade or business of catching fish, or, generally, the cash paid from a notional principal contract to an individual, partnership, or estate; any fishing boat proceeds, or gross proceeds of $600, or more paid to an attorney during the year. Also, use Form 1099-MISC to report that you made direct sales of at least $5,000 of consumer products to a buyer for resale anywhere other than a permanent retail establishment."

Likewise, if you pay another self-employed person for contract services and you pay them $600 or more you are required to send them a 1099- MISC and send a copy to the IRS. Generally, you must furnish Form 1099-MISC by January 31st, or the next business day if that date falls on a weekend. You can obtain the U.S. Internal Revenue Service publication called, *General Instructions for Certain Information Returns*, for more details by visiting www.IRS.gov.

1099-K

The U.S. Internal Revenue Service states that "a payment settlement entity (PSE) must file Form 1099-K for payments made in settlement of reportable payment transactions for each calendar year. A PSE makes a payment in settlement of a reportable payment transaction, that is, any payment card or third party network transaction, if the PSE submits the instruction to transfer funds to the account of the participating payee to settle the reportable payment transaction."

This means that if you received revenues from your online sales—settled through an online third party network or any sales settled through a card payment provider, it must be reported on form 1099-K. For Example, if you collect sales revenues through online payment processing companies like Paypal and Propay, these third party networks are required to send you and the U.S. Internal Revenue Service a copy of all your proceeds (gross). This way the U.S. Internal Revenue Service has a record of it, but this only applies to businesses with gross amount of total reportable payment transactions that exceed $20,000, and the number of transactions exceeds 200. Generally, you should receive Form 1099-K by the January 31st, or the next business day if the 31st falls on a weekend. See the U.S. Internal Revenue Service publication called, *General Instructions for Certain Information Returns.*

PROFITABILITY

Small business owners sometimes misinterpret the difference between revenue and profit. As a matter of fact, when the business funds get low, many of them assume that they need more revenue without realizing that what they truly need is a Profit. Out of desperation they hire a business coach to teach them how to get more revenues, but they can't even afford the coach. Now they have depleted what funds they have left, and within a few months find themselves in the same cash shortage scenario. There is a big difference between Revenue and Profit, sometimes referred to as Income by many business owners. So what's the difference? Before we take a closer look, study the formula in figure 7.1, this is the profit equation.

REVENUES - EXPENSES = PROFIT

Revenue: This is what you earned from sales or services you provided. It's the reason you did all that marketing.	**Expenses:** This is what you spent your money on to keep the business going. Like rent, supplies, inventory, etc.	**Profit:** This is what you have left after you paid all your bills. This is what you put back into your business to keep it growing.

Figure 7.1 the profit equation.

Here is the difference. Revenue is what the U.S. Internal Revenue Service calls *Gross Income*, but in the business world it's called revenue, this is money you generated from performing services or selling products. This is the end result of your successful marketing. It is sometimes also called *Gross Sales*. This is what you collected from your customers before any bills are paid. Profit is what you have left in your bank account after all your business expenses are paid, both operating and administrative expenses. For example, if you collected $10,000 in sales revenue from your customers for the month and deposited the money into your business bank account, you are not free to use this money for whatever you want just yet. You must cover your monthly bills first. Let's assume your monthly bills are rent $1,500, electricity and water $500, credit card monthly charges for office supplies $200, part time assistant $1,000, internet, phone and cable service bundle $200, marketing $300, merchandise bought from suppliers—paid every thirty days $2,500, that's a total of $6,200. Once these bills are paid, you will have $3,800 left over, that's 38% of revenues left over as profit, $3,800 ÷ $10,000 = 38%.

Now, normally what you should do is apply some of the profits back into the business. Generally, the best use would be to apply it towards marketing to keep attracting customers into your business—that's if you have no other priorities. The reasoning behind this decision is that as a self-employed individual your first goal should be to grow and build up your customer base so that you can generate lots of revenue. As you get more customers and sales revenue grows, you can now start hiring employees, a virtual service, or get other independent contractors to work for you. This is the only way for you to avoid getting burnout, no one business owner can do everything by themselves. You need people to help you take your business to the next level. If you do not plan for this and your business gets really busy with customer demands, you will eventually burnout from over working. You have to meet customer's requests, administrative demands, accounting and tax responsibilities, business planning and strategy task, family responsibilities, and so much more. So you see, you will need someone to help you at some point. Also, as a client of mine once noted—you'll never make any real money until you hire people to work for you.

HOW DO YOU BECOME PROFITABLE?

Getting back to the 38% of revenues left over as profit, many self- employed people unfortunately would not be in a position to apply their profits towards business growth or even save for future use. This is because many self-employed people have no other income but their business income, and so they use the profits for their living expenses. This is the main reason that most business owners appear not to be profitable. They have profits in the business, but they also have to pay for their personal rent or mortgage, car note, credit cards, groceries, children's needs, medical insurance (if they can afford it), retirement savings, clothing, school loans, and taxes. Now based on the $3,800 left over in the business, if you were to take this money and use it to cover the personal expenses listed above, it may not be enough. There is nothing wrong with using some of the profits for personal use, after all you are earning a living; the difference is that you work for yourself. However, what makes so many self-employed people feel sometimes like they perhaps should not have left their jobs, is that they work hard to bring in customers, manage their business and keep up their personal lives, but it seems like there's just not enough money to relief the stresses of life. As a matter of fact, many self-employed people are earning more than they were getting at their previous jobs, but the revenue must cover both the business and their household expenses.

To overcome this challenge business owners have to purposely plan to be profitable and live frugal—very frugal. The rationale by many self- employed people to avoid living frugal is that they need to enjoy because life is short and that one must live in the moment. Some even feel like they have struggled financially for enough years and they are tired of budgets, and not being able to do the things they want to do. But living frugal does not mean you have to live in a pig pen, it means that you spend your money wisely and buy only the essentials. If you truly believe in what you doing, then down size so that you will have more disposable income. For example, get rid of the car payment if it's depleting your funds, move to a smaller or less expensive apartment in a neighborhood that you like, cut down the grocery bill, find cheaper ways to do things. For your business offer the best your money can buy for your customers because this is the investment that will actually get you the sweet returns, and put you on a path to eventually buy whatever you want.

The sacrifice of living frugal is nothing compared to the rewards. This is part of what separates those who make it to success from those who don't. For every decision you make there is a consequence. As a self-employed business owner you live frugal because you want to have enough money in your bank account so that you do not put yourself in a distressing situation that will lead to the loss of your business or your livelihood. You want peace of mind, the ability to choose, to sleep peacefully at night, to not depend on anyone, to experience success and eventually show others how to do the same. You do it for your children, do it for dignity, do it for you. We will examine how to accomplish the balance between business and personal in chapter nine.

Recalling the profit equation, *Revenues minus Expenses equals Profit,* your strategy to maximize profit is to spend less than what you bring in. As you can see in the equation expenses are subtracted from revenues, so the less you subtract the more you will keep. The more you keep in your bank account the more you will have to reinvest in your business and allocate towards other investments to grow your money. The key to subtracting less money to cover expenses is to control cost, and to control cost successfully; you will have to apply cost management strategies, which is revealed in chapter eight—let's take a look at these now.

LESSONS IN BUSINESS

8

THE THREE
MOST IMPORTANT BUSINESS COST

"If you want to thrive in today's economy, you must challenge the status quo and get the financial education necessary to succeed.

~ ROBERT KIYOSAKI

It takes money to operate a business, but it takes discipline to make it profitable. Imbedded into the clear-cut calculation of profitability is the necessity to control cost if you want to make a profit—a task that is easier said than done. In this section you will learn the three most important business cost categories that every self- employed business owner must learn to control and the strategies for controlling them. It would be nice to keep all the revenues generated from the sales of products and services, but as noted earlier—it takes money to operate a business. This means that to keep a business going, the owner will need to invest money to run it. This money is commonly referred to as *Working Capital*.

However, working capital for a self-employed business owner comes in three different forms (a) directly from the owner's savings, (b) business profits reinvested back into the business, or (c) borrowed money from a bank or private lender. Keep in mind that a self- employed business owner is not a legally recognized business separate from its owner, so his or her access to funding is usually limited to these three options even though there are other funding options for businesses. Of these three choices the most preferred option is business profits reinvested back into the business. This is because one sign of a thriving business is its ability to sustain itself. If a business owner has to keep pulling funds from a personal savings account to keep the business running, then it's a sign that there is a problem with generating revenues or that there are issues in the management of the business costs. Likewise, if a business owner has to take a business loan to simply cover the day-to-day business expenses of his or her operations, then there is a cash flow problem. To pay this money back to the lender, the business owner will need to increase revenues and carefully manage the use of cash to cover expenses in order to make a profit and also pay the debt back. Let's look at an example of this situation using the profit equation. In the figure 8.1 below we see a business owner whose revenues from sales are $50,000 and expenses are $60,000 for a one year period. Therefore expenses exceed revenues by $10,000 as shown in figure 8.1.

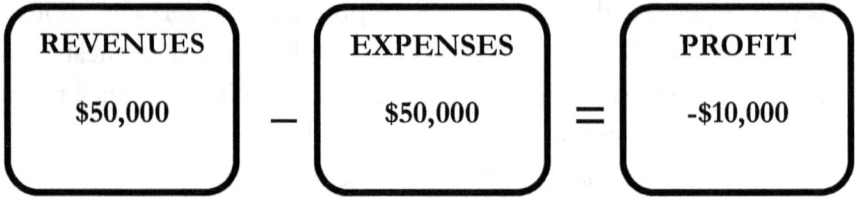

REVENUES		EXPENSES		PROFIT
$50,000	—	$50,000	=	-$10,000

Figure 8.1.

Technically, the $10,000 loss means that there was not enough money to cover the expenses. So, how were the bills paid if there was not enough money and where did the money come from? Well, the $10,000 of bills may not have been paid. This business owner would have had to take out a $10,000 loan from the bank, pull from personal funds, or borrow from family to help pay the business expenses. In this scenario we will assume that the money was borrowed from a bank, and the loan was just enough to cover the $10,000 cash shortage. So, the end result was zero profit and a new $10,000 debt. Assuming the loan was to be paid back in the current period, figure 8.3 shows what would have to happen.

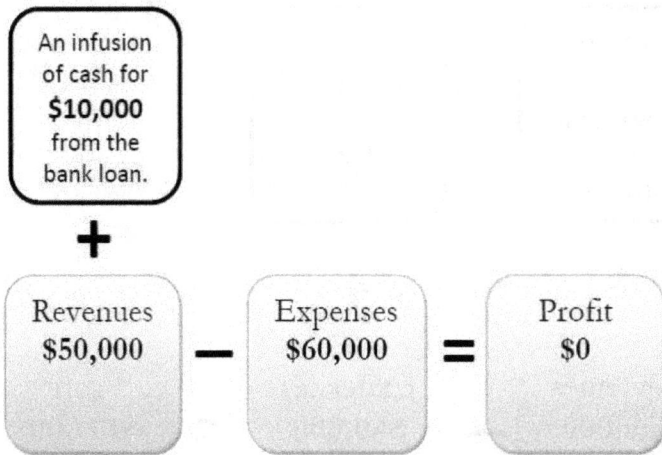

Figure 8.2

In order for the business owner to pay back the bank loan of $10,000, the ideal situation would be to increase revenues. However, to increase revenues the business owner needs to either get more customers, increase prices, or get more streams of income. In this scenario the business owner decided to get more customers.

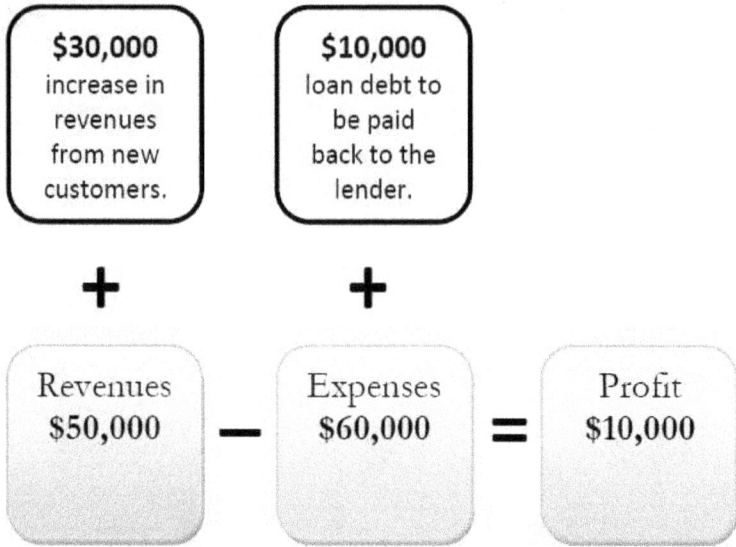

Figure 8.3

Assuming the business owner was able to increase revenues by an additional $30,000, revenues for the year would be $80,000 instead of $50,000; then paying off the $10,000 loan and $60,000 in expenses would result in a profit of $10,000. The purpose of this example is to show you that you should not rely on loans to cover basic operating expenses as there is no guarantee that you will raise enough money to cover the debt and still turn a profit—well, not without a really good plan. Instead, business owners should focus on controlling expenses, but continue to market their business to increase revenues.

WHAT ARE THE THREE COST CATEGORIES?

In order to understand the three cost categories, it may help to understand the three requirements that every business must carry out at a minimum to keep the business moving in the right direction. First, a business needs to grow, and in order to grow among other things there must be marketing. Second, a business must be able to carry out its day-to-day basic functions to keep it going. Third, a business needs to adhere to regulatory requirements. Reflecting on these three requirements, we can then say that business cost are divided up into (a) Cost of growth, (b) Cost of operations, and (c) Cost of compliance. Understanding these basic cost categories will help you as a self-employed individual to prioritize your costs and monitor your spending behaviors. This knowledge becomes very important when you need to decide what should be paid first when there's not enough money for the month, or what should be kept if the budget needs to be trimmed. Controlling cost is the biggest challenge for many business owners. Even the management teams of major corporations are always seeking ways to control cost so that they can show more profits (the bottom line) for their stockholders and prospective investors. But it is not enough to just know what strategies are available, to be effective you have to understand why you are doing what you are doing. A good starting point would be to get a clear understand of the three cost categories.

THE COST OF GROWTH

Imagine getting a text message from a business affiliate to participate in an event being hosted by your local business chamber, and for a set price your business will be included in the marketing materials. This is your opportunity for exposure and to get new customers on the day of the event—totally unplanned, what would you do?

Usually, when most self-employed individuals look at the cost associate with running a business, all they see is the costs or expenses required to keep the business going. But if one takes a closer look, many of these costs are actually investments. Every business owner wants their business to grow, but what does business growth really mean? When people say they want their business to grow, what they are really saying is that they want to increase revenues and profits so that they can see the vision they have for their company and personal life materialize. With the growth in revenues they can hire more people to work in the business which will increase the potential for greater profits, and with the increase in profits they are more likely to attain financial independence. So, why think of cost as an investment?

The *costs of growth* are those costs which are necessary to generate revenues. These costs can be controlled by the business owner and it should be thought of more as an investment. Typically, when a person buys the stock of another company as an investment, they are giving money to that company in exchange for an ownership percentage. They are exercising confidence in that entity, and hoping that the management of that company will continue to make decisions that will result in the company making really good returns so that they will get a return on their investment—Dividends. Well, those managers and executives have to put that money to good use in order to ensure that the company thrives. Investing in things like research and development, marketing, a competent workforce, various community efforts, efficient technology, and security. These few items mentioned are all examples of cost incurred by the company to help the company grow, but the money was not disbursed blindly. There was a lot of planning and inquiry that took place before deciding where to allocate the company funds. Likewise, as a self-employed individual and business owner it is very important that you identify what will help your business to grow, and assess how effective it will be in helping you achieve "that specific goal" before you spend money on it.

For example, if you are thinking of hiring an assistant, getting a new phone, and a website but you are on a tight budget, you will have to prioritize what to spend your money on. All things being fair, getting a new phone will not help you get new customers, and it will not help you bring money into the business, so there is no real justification for getting a new phone—you can wait and get the phone at a later time. Deciding between the website and the assistant will depend on what type of business you have. If you run an e-business the decision is clear and the website should get priority because this is what your business model is based on. However, if you operate a business requiring you to meet with clients in person or you travel often, the assistant will help you manage your business affairs more effectively so that you can take on more clients and offer them exceptional service. This will bring in more money and help you grow your business. Even if you have adequate funds in your bank account, sometimes you will have to put off things that you want for your business till a later time in order to have money for unplanned situations. Focus on your business needs and once you get some additional funds in, you can then get those things that you would like to have—like a new phone for instance. Practice delayed gratification, increase your retained funds and use that money to create more money, this is the starting point for wealth creation. But we will discuss more of that in chapter nine.

CONSIDER THIS...

Every business owner should allocate a portion of their budget towards activities that will help bring customers to their business. This should be purposeful in planning, remember without customers you have no business. It's always amazing to see how many people start a business and just assume that the customers will come. Such a chance may work for businesses like restaurants and boutiques located in a busy area. But with so many choices for the consumers to choose from, not advertising could very well mean that money is being left on the table—too risky. Your business model and marketing plan will help you narrow your marketing focus so that you can use the most effective tools for your business type, this way you can achieve your goals.

THE COST OF OPERATIONS

Suppose you are running a local restaurant in town serving breakfast and lunch sandwiches to working professionals in the area. During the busy lunch rush you realize that you are out of an item used in preparing a particular sandwich, do you send someone to go get the item right away or tell the customer you are out?

The biggest cost for most self-employed people is the cost of operations. Although, this cost can be controlled, doing so requires focus. There are self-employed individuals who rarely consider that they actually have control over their expenses, that they can control the timing of when those expenses are paid and how much is paid. Another issue is overspending, this is a leading cause of cash shortage, but the main cause of overspending is unplanned purchases. If you are going to be profitable you will have to discipline yourself, know what cost are essential, and use a budget to help you monitor your cost. As matter of fact, especially in the early stages of your business, know that it's okay to say *"no"* to any cost that does not add value to your business, will not help you get more customers, or keep you in compliance with government regulations. This is because in order for you to be profitable you must spend less than what you bring in, and to do that you have to know what's necessary and what's not. Solopreneurs can easily lose control when they desire certain things, but rationalize in favor of what they want vs. need. I am not saying that you should not get what you want, but rather that you should get what you want from among the choices available for what you need. For example, if you run a Day Care at home and you need toys for the children, when you get to the store you notice that you have the option to buy inexpensive toys that just keep the kids active, but you would rather have educational games and videos even though they cost more—buy it. Your clients, who are the children's parents, will very much appreciate *the added value* your service offers.

How do I control my operating expenses?

Perhaps you've tried managing your expenses but gave up because it was too overwhelming. Maybe you figured out a system and it works for you, but there's hardly any money left over at the end of the month. Well, *timing* plays a big role helping you control cost and you have to implement a cash management system that will work for you. This system should be part of your operating plan, it's how you do things in your business to keep it going. For example, most bills are due at the end or the beginning of the month. Some companies will bill in the middle of the month or offer you a predetermined amount of time to get your payments in, like thirty days, fifteen days or ten days. But, it's your business—you are in control, so you should decide how you want your billing structured. If a company's payment plan does not work for you don't use them, remember *it's your business*, not theirs. This is the power you have—to choose how you *operate* your business. Let's look at Rafael's business and personal scenario as an example to help you understand how this works.

Rafael's Scenario

BALANCING BUSINESS AND PERSONAL FINANCE

Rafael runs a service business, his monthly revenues are $10,000 (cash, credit card, checks and online payment options). Due to the nature of his business, 30 percent ($3,000) of this amount comes in at the begging of the month, 50 percent ($5,000) around the middle of the month and 20 percent ($2,000) comes in closer to the end of the month. This is the pattern every month regardless of how much revenue he makes.

His monthly business expenses comes to $6,000 as listed below:
- Business Rent $1,500–due on the 1st of the month.
- Utilities $300–due on the 15th of the month.
- Phone and Internet bundled services $200–due on the 1st
- Office Assistant $2,000–paid the 1st and the 15th of the month.
- Marketing Campaign $1,000–due on the 1st of the month.
- Office supplies and other expenses $1,000—purchased throughout the month.

His monthly **Personal** expenses are $2,500 as listed below:
- ✓ Personal Rent or Mortgage (insurance included) $1,000–due on the 1st of the month.
- ✓ Car Note #1 $500–due on the 15th of the month.
- ✓ Car Note #2 Spouse $300–due on the 15th of the month.
- ✓ Food and other living needs $300–purchased throughout the month.
- ✓ Children's needs and other expenses $400–paid throughout the month.

Considering the circumstances, Rafael seems to be in a really tight situation. If he makes the wrong moves he could very well find himself in a financial bind, but if he makes the right moves he will be on his way to financial strength.

So how should Rafael manage his operating cost?

Remember, Rafael is self–employed so whatever profit he has a portion of it is used for his personal expenses. His business expenses that are due on the 1st of the month add up to $3,700 and his personal expenses add up to $1,000, but he only collected $3,000 at the begging of the month. So based on the facts provided, Rafael has $4,700 in expenses he has to pay with only $3,000. Looking at the month's activity in its entirety we can see that Rafael is actually able to pay both his business and personal bills and still have $1,500 left in his bank account at the end of the month. But in reality as with many self–employed people, customers do not always pay when they are supposed to and bill are not always due when you actually have most of your revenues in– this is the "timing" issue. So Rafael will have to strategize to make this work every month until he has enough savings put aside to exercise more options available to him.

First Assumption

Starting with the $4,700 in bills due at the beginning of the month, Rafael will have to prioritize what gets paid first. His business rent is a necessary cost that goes towards providing him with a place where he can work, meet with clients–in other words his office provides him the opportunity to make money. If Rafael does not pay his rent that opportunity will be snatched from him, so he pays the $1,500 rent first. His home is part of his livelihood; it's where he and his family take shelter, so if he does not pay he will be homeless, therefore this gets paid immediately also. Third in line should be his office assistant because his assistant earned this money working with him in good faith and it is a legal obligation, besides his assistant helps him to make money also. That's $3,500 dollars so far without the phone and internet bundle cost or his marketing campaign paid; and he only had $3,000 coming in at the beginning of the month? Sure, but in order to make it work, Rafael would have had to save the $2,000 that came in toward the end of the month–that would have been at least one week before the beginning of the month. In addition, rents are usually a known fixed payment under contract, so every month it's the same amount.

As with every self-employed person, Rafael knew that he had two rents to pay, so part of his plan was to save the $2,000 that came in at the end of the month for the bills that he would have to pay at the beginning of the month. The problem that most self-employed business owners have is spending money left over on unnecessary items just because there are very little or no bills due at that time. Don't put yourself in a cash shortage crisis—save that money so you won't stress out when your bill are due.

Second Assumption

But, what if Rafael really didn't have money saved to help cover his bills at the beginning of the month? Well, he would have to pay his business rent first since it is a higher cost and his place of business. If he paid it late, as with most lease agreements a percentage of the rent plus a late fee would be assessed—this would create a bigger debt. He would then pay his office assistant, being a responsible business person who shows appreciation for the people who help him make money. As for his monthly marketing campaign, and phone and internet bundle, Rafael would have to call both companies and make arrangements for an alternative payment dates. His personal rent would have to be paid late because the late charges on it are lower, and the landlord or bank if it was a mortgage, is sometimes more flexible on personal leases. But Rafael would need to save whatever unused money he has remaining from the $3,000 he collected from his clients to make the plan work and immediately pay his personal rent and other business debts as soon as he gathers enough money. Rafael would use this same process of prioritizing to ensure all his other bills are paid during the middle of the month and at the end of the month.

There's $1,500 left over for the month
what should this money be used for?

Nothing. Rafael should save this money in his business bank account, because he is on a budget and wants to see his business grow. The money should be set aside for emergencies. In addition, the revenues for the next month may not be as much as the previous month, a wise business person never assumes that business will be great every month. In business, some months are busy and some months are very slow. One should always be prepared to sustain their business in the tough times, the main reasons some businesses don't survive the tough times is poor money management skills and lack of marketing.

What else can Rafael do as a business owner to manage his operations wisely?

In addition to working with an operating budget to help him monitor his business costs and saving as much of the profits as possible, Rafael should also review his budget to see if all his expenses are necessary. If he realizes that there are expenses that he does not need to operate his business, he simply makes a decision to stop incurring that expense. He should also see if he can negotiate better terms with his current suppliers and service providers, if not, he should seek out new suppliers and service providers that will offer him better payment terms and lower pricing so that he can realize more profits. If he is already receiving the lower price point, then he can choose to change how he provides services to his clients, order less supplies, reduce labor cost or cut back any other operating or administrative costs he has. There's always a solvable solution, the challenge is to find the courage to change, so that you can get the result you want.

The example using Rafael's scenario was a glance at what self-employed people can do to manage, grow and sustain their businesses. But there are a few other time tested business operating techniques that can be used to control business cost, we will examine these techniques using the *Cash Flow* statement.

What is a Cash Flow Statement?

To help you understand the significance of the Cash Flow statement, let's take a look at the statements that make up the Financial Statements. There are four primary Financial Statements: the Income Statement also referred to as the *Profit and Loss*, the *Balance Sheet*, the *Retained Earnings* statement, and the Cash Flow statement. In this book we have been using the term *profit and loss* instead of *income statement*, as it is the term mostly use by self-employed individuals. *The profit and loss* statement is a history of your revenues and expenses summarized for a particular period. It shows how much money you made in your business and how much money you spent to operate your business. If you have money left over after paying your expenses you make a profit and if you spent more than you made in revenues running your business then you will have a Loss. The profit and loss statement is good for assessing how well you are managing your business operations. The *balance sheet* is a snapshot of what the business owns (assets), what it owes (liabilities) and if all the business debts were paid off, how much of the earning would be retained by the business owner (owner's equity). Because some of the amounts listed in the *assets* section of the balance sheet is listed at cost, if all the business debts were paid the equity section would not reflect accurately the amount money that the business owner is entitled to. This is because some of the assets may have depreciated (declined) in value, while some may have appreciated (increased) in value. The equity section of the balance sheet shows how much money was invested into the business by the owner, how much of the profits were retained by the business and how much money has been drawn out by the business owner. The statement of *retained earnings* shows how much money has been retained by the business to date.

The cash flow statement shows the movement of cash through the business. The movement of cash through the business will usually impact at least one of the three primary business activities, Operating, Investing and Financing. The cash flow statement shows how much cash was used to run the operations of the business and how much cash was collected from sales and services. It also shows, from the cash in the business how much was used to buy equipment, real estate or other investments, as well as how much was received from the various investment made by the business. Lastly, it shows how much cash was paid or collected for debt financing. The cash flow statement is perhaps the most important financial statement when looking to see how well a business owner operates their business and manages their cash. One reason is because, unlike the profit and loss statement, the cash flow statement does not include services or sales provided on credit. When a business has performed a service or sold an item on credit there is no guarantee of ever collecting the cash. The credit sales is included on the profit and loss statement to capture the total revenue for the period, but it is excluded from the cash flow statement because the money has not been received yet. The opposite also applies, sometimes you have expenses that are listed on your profit and loss statement, but will not appear on the cash flow statement because it was not paid, or it is not a real cash expense. Some examples of this expense type are depreciation and bad debt expense, both are not cash expenses.

How do I manage my cash efficiently?

As mentioned previously, self-employed individuals can implement time tested business operating techniques to help control cost so that they can grow and sustain their businesses. Keeping in mind what you have now learned about the cash flow statement, we can now take a deeper look at a few of these effective techniques. We will focus our attention on what impacts cash the most—cash collections and cash payments.

Cash Collections

Remember that the cash flow statement shows the movement of cash throughout the business, as such non–cash expenses and revenues from sales or services offered on credit are not included on the statement. To improve cash flow you want to convert those credit sales and services to cash. To help you with this you will need some structure, so make sure you have a credit policy. Your credit policy is a written description of your company's guidelines on providing products or services on credit. Depending on your specific business, whether you are selling a product or providing a service, create a customer version and make sure your customers know about it. For example, you can put it in a frame and hang it on the wall, or have a one page explanation and include it with the client's paperwork and have them initial it. Also, for your business staff, document your procedures and identify your step-by-step process from extending credit to following up with your customers to collect payment. For instance, you need to indicate when you are going to send out the first reminder after the invoice has been issued or if you offered a split payment when the follow up payment will be charged and what you will do if a credit or debit card is declined. Offering sales and services on Credit is usually established by many businesses to open up opportunities to increase sales revenue. We know that cash is king, whether you are dealing with consumers or doing business to business transactions—cash is king, so in order to get more sales, you offer credit terms that are appropriate for your industry to help increase your sales revenue. But you need to have procedures in place so that you strengthen your ability to convert those credit sales to cash collections. Listed below are some solutions to help you convert your credit sales to cash quicker.

CONVERTING YOUR CREDIT SALES TO CASH

Focus on Collecting Large Balances.
It's better that you spend time and energy on the large balances. For example if you have $50 owed to you by one client and $350 owed to you by another, focus on collecting the $350, but do not ignore the $50.

Get your team involved in the process.
If you have a staff member or two who helps you with sales, customer service, bookkeeping, or speaks with your customers as part of their work, make it part of their routine to follow up with the customer about a past due bill. Whether they are offering additional services or responding to a customer inquiry, have your staff follow up with them about the payment in a friendly manner.

Offer terms that will encourage savings.
We all like saving money and so do your customers. You may be able to encourage your customers to get their bill paid early by offering them a discount if they pay by a certain date. For example, you pay 10% less if paid within ten days, or the full amount is due if paid beyond that time frame. Additionally, you may assess a late charge or a fee if the bill is paid late.

Help your customer find a solution.
In a friendly manner, find out what's preventing them from getting their bills paid and help your customer come up with a workable solution. Sometimes, when you talk to them you realize that there are real issues, so you can use the opportunity to offer a solution that will help them and get you paid.

Be flexible.
Sometimes an arrangement may not be within your business procedures, but due to your valued client's situation they may ask for a certain arrangement that works for them financially. Your goal is to collect your money, so you may want to consider the alternative arrangement offered by your customer.

Negotiate.
If the situation seems hopeless, then negotiate to collect at least enough to cover your cost and write off the uncollected portion as a Bad Debt expense.

THE CAT AND MOUSE CHASE

Some self-employed individuals get caught in a cat and mouse chase, driving miles to pick up a check. You are scheduling meeting times to get paid and then the appointment gets cancelled like two or three times because that client of yours has more important business to take care of. That's not flexibility, you are being disrespected. Clients like this have no respect for you, their behavior implies that you are not a priority to them, you are insignificant and you need them to help your business generate revenues more than they need your services. Basically, when they are available to pay you, that's when you will get paid. This behavior is exhausting, frustrating and hurting your business. The time you could spend wowing other customers, you are spending it on this customer and still not getting paid for your time. In addition, you are spending more money on fuel, and dispensing energy that should be used to focus on other important tasks.

If you find yourself in this type of a situation dropped the client, but be strategic about it. Be patient don't do any other work until you get your money then discontinue services to the client. Some self-employed people encounter this with a high paying client and are putting up with this inconsiderate behavior just for the money. It's a tough decision but you must let them go, you do not deserve the frustration, additional cost, and stress. Free yourself and make room for other clients. New clients that will treat your business with respect will come.

One of the best efforts you can make is to reduce or eliminate having receivables as much as possible and focus on increasing cash collections at the point of sale (POS).

POS STRATEGIES TO INCREASE CASH COLLECTIONS

50 percent now and 50 percent upon completion.

This is the half now, half later option. If you provide services, do not start working on any project until you collect at least half the estimate or half the service fees upfront, and the rest will be due upon completion of the work, and if you do not collect your payment, do not deliver the work.

Percentage-of-Completion.

This method is often used in the construction industry for revenue recognition on large long term projects. But you can apply the same method in your business for collection purposes only. Even if you are providing services. Set up a system so that as you advance through the project phases you bill the client for payment to continue the next phase. For example, let's say you are a painter, and you've been hired to paint the exterior and interior of a local school. It's going to take a few weeks for you and your team to get the work done. You can break the project up into phases, let's assume you collect 33 percent upfront to start the work, another 33 percent before moving to the next phase, and the remainder before the work is complete. It's a fair payment method for both you and the client, particularly on jobs where the client does not want to pay everything upfront. This method is also a great way to collect money to fund the project like buying materials, pay for the labor cost and other miscellaneous expenses without having to use money retained in the company.

Collect all the money upfront.
With this option no service is provided unless payment is received.

Pre-payment arrangements.
Make payment arrangements with your clients, but either (a) collect a post-dated check for the amounts due, or (b) get a credit card preauthorization on file for the agreed upon charge dates.

Get automated.
There are several companies and e-commerce businesses that can provide you with a platform where your clients can pay online. In addition, you can have your collection process automated. As with anything else it will cost some money, but it may be worth it to have this type of service. With this service you and your team can focus more on the business, enhancing your customer's experience, and focus on income generating and brand building activities.

CASH PAYMENTS

Equally important to help you grow and sustain your business is managing your cash payments appropriately. Every business owner knows that cash is king, so implementing a cash disbursement strategy will help you to maintain control over your cash. The purpose of having a cash payment strategy is to give yourself the opportunity to control the outflow of cash from the business, so that you have enough money left in the business to keep the operations going. A cash payment strategy should not be implemented deliberately to prolong payments to suppliers and service providers so that you have enough money for your own personal desires. Reputation of business owners eventually spreads throughout the community, and as a self-employed person if you purposefully withhold payment from suppliers, employees, contractors or others, you may find it hard to build trust, get local business affiliates or even obtain credit. If you are short on cash and cannot pay your liabilities in a timely manner, communicate with the people or companies that you owe. It may feel uncomfortable and even somewhat embarrassing, but swallow your pride and do not be afraid to let them know respectfully that you can't make the payment right now. You will obtain more respect, and offer creditors peace of mind by keeping them informed. Also, if the debt is large you may benefit from making small payments over a period of time, this way they will see your sincere effort to get your liabilities paid.

There may be times, when you just don't have the money to pay anything. Perhaps it's because sales are really low, collections are slow coming in or you simply did not budget appropriately. Things happen and people makes mistakes at times, the lessons learned are hard ones that can really become a humbling experience. But pull yourself together! Your situation is not unique. It will take some time, months or even years for larger debts to be paid. It will also require some discipline, focus, and strategic planning on your part to dig yourself out of a hole. Surviving this short episode in life may mean that you have to get expert help, restructure your business, intensify your marketing campaign to get more customers, or get on a really strict cash budget. In this type of situation you are going to have to act quickly to implement an action plan to pay off debts. Generally, the only way to get your liabilities paid is with money, and to get money as a self-employed person you must work for it. This is why having multiple streams of revenue is important, it can help to lessen the stress of trying to figure out where money will come from. As your business grows you should begin to transition to having your money work for you, by employing people and integrating a system where your business begins to depend less on you having to be present at all times in order for it to function. If you are used to paying the full balance of your bills right when it's due, when you are experiencing a cash shortage you have to manage your funds very strategically; if not you will find yourself not being able to take care of your daily business responsibilities or take advantage of other opportunities. Listed below are some cash payment solutions to maintain control of your operations.

STRATEGIES TO CONTROL CASH PAYMENTS

Choose the best payment term.
Take full advantage of creditor payment terms. Most suppliers or service providers give thirty days to get the payments in. On the other hand you may consider taking advantage of discounts from paying early this way you can keep more money in the business.

Automate fixed payments.
For fixed monthly payments, to make your life easier set up automatic payments on dates that work well for your business cash flow. This way you know exactly when the payments are coming out and you can plan for it.

Choose your own dates.
You may want to avoid any auto payments if the amounts are different from month to month so that you can control when the payment goes out. This will give you peace of mind, allowing you pay the bills when you have the money. This will also help you avoid any overdraft fees that you may have incurred if the funds are not yet in your account. This may work better with a national or global company service provider that offers more flexibility.

Ask for what you need.
When you are running a limited business budget you may want to ask for alternative payment arrangements, like extended terms or ask to pay on the date when you know you'll get your funds. Especially if you are receiving services from another small business, most people are willing to be a little flexible if you are bringing in good business to them.

Find another supplier.
If your current service provider or supplier does not offer terms that work for you, it's okay to switch to another supplier. But not at the cost of quality, so if you are considering switching to a new service provider or supplier assess the pros and cons carefully.

THE COST OF COMPLIANCE

So far you have learned about the importance of the cost of growth and how to control your cost of operations, now we will take a look at the cost of compliance. Part of your responsibility as a business owner is to know what the governing authorities in your industry, country and state require of you in order for you to operate a business. Many times self-employed individuals focus more on the creation of the business and leave out the regulatory side of owing a business. As long as you are operating a business you will have some cost of compliance. The cost of compliance includes the various regulatory related costs that you incur as a result of being in business. Your regulatory cost may include taxes, licensing, and continuing education requirements. In many cases, these cost are paid annually, and are not optional. Make sure that you know what these costs are and include them in your budget. Taxes to be paid are not usually known until the tax forms are filed, but you can estimate how much you may have to pay based on the previous years' amounts and set aside the money in your savings account.

If you are a new business, you can use tax tables to estimate an amount based on expected income or set aside a percentage of your income habitually on a monthly or quarterly basis to meet your compliance requirements. If you happen to come up short because your estimate was off, you can add the difference when the tax forms are filed, or expect a refund if you overpaid. You may also choose to have the overpayment applied to the subsequent years' taxes. Cost associated with staying in compliance with regulatory authorities are not a secret, and should be planned for in advance to avoid incurring unwarranted penalties, losing your business, being denied the right to operate a business or possibly losing your assets to settle a government debt.

GENERAL TIPS TO KEEP COST UNDER CONTROL

- Share office space with those in a related industry as yours, this way you are sharing the cost of the business rent with other professionals and getting the referrals also. For example, if you are a business attorney you can share your office space with an accountant, and an insurance agent.

- Choose the most fitting payroll dates for your business. As a self- employed business owner you need structure, but one that you can manage appropriately. You can choose to pay your staff or contractors monthly, semi-monthly or weekly. Monthly or semi- monthly may offer you more room to get cash into the business so that you can comfortably meet your obligations.

- Buy supplies in small quantities instead of overstocking, most supplies take a while to get used. You can buy what you need or just enough for the month and keep more cash in the business. Sometimes buying in bulk offers savings, but you must assess if buying more supplies now which can lead to a cash shortage is worth saving a few dollars in the long run.

- Inventory quantities should also be kept low. Buying in large amounts may not be wise if the turnover is not high. Keeping the inventory quantities low will not only keep more money in the business, but it can also help to reduce loss of inventory due waste resulting from expired dates, damaged goods and spoilage.

- Run tax projections three to four months ahead to give you the opportunity to see how much you may be obligated to pay. With this insightful information you can implement tax saving strategies before the filing season starts and eliminate surprises.

- Monitor bank balances daily by setting up online banking. Pay attention to what checks are pending payment, or debit items that may be posting at a later date, so that you can ensure that you have enough money in your bank account. Always review bank transactions for accuracy and know what fees your bank is charging and when they are due. A bank charge can over draw an account and cause a payment to be rejected. Set up two checking accounts, one as a cash control account which will be used primarily to pay bills and the other to act as a deposit account and overdraft protection in case you don't get to transfer funds due to a busy schedule. In your cash control checking account, keep just enough money to cover bills and miscellaneous items. Transfer any excess cash after your bills and miscellaneous items have been accounted for to your savings account and keep your business savings unlinked and off limits. This will help you avoid unplanned purchases because you will not have easy access to your savings, and it will help to safeguard against the loss of money due to debit card, check or electronic funds transfer fraud. If you have any unauthorized transaction in your account notify your banker quickly, but getting your money back may take months because of the time involved in the investigative process.

As a self-employed business owner you have the ability to use your financial data to control your business outcomes. When you do not take control, you are releasing that power to chance; to the unknown. You have the authority over your business to control your costs so that you can be profitable and grow your business. You are the one to decide what is important and what is not; it is your business and what your business becomes is a reflection of the choices you have made as a business owner. Even if you have been pushed into a difficult situation, you can still choose how you will respond to the situation. Never let anyone force you into buying what you do not want, review your financial plans and operating budget regularly to help you stay focused on your goals. It will require discipline and tenacity to achieve result, but it will be well worth it in the long run. In addition, when there are changes in the economy or consumer behavior you will be able to make the needed adjustment and sustain your business.

IDENTIFYING AND CORRECTING
A FAILING BUSINESS

You are constantly pulling cash from your personal funds.

This usually happens when you are undercapitalized, it's a sign that you cannot afford to pay your current operating expenses. Current operating expenses are the expenses incurred in carrying out your day-to-day business activities. These expenses include payroll, rent, basic repairs, supplies needed for the office, insurance, bookkeeping and accounting fees, utilities, etc. Constantly pulling money from your personal funds is not healthy, because a business needs to be able to generate enough money to keep it going. To turn this situation around create an operating budget to help you monitor your expenses. Be realistic when creating your budget and try your best to stay as close as possible to the spending limits on your budget. Start by estimating your monthly revenues, use your prior month's sales as a reference, and then take your monthly expenses and subtract that number from your estimated revenues. If you have a money left over once you subtract your expenses, then you will have a profit—set this excess aside for future needs. Monitor your bank account daily, if you don't have online banking sign up for it so you can keep an eye on your cash daily.

Establish a rule that requires your bank account to have a certain minimum balance at all times, this should ensure that you always have funds. Open a business savings and allocate a certain portion of your revenues to your savings, this way you can transfer money when needed. You can also use your accountant as a responsibility partner to help you stay accountable.

High Sales, Low Cash.

The cause of high sales, low cash is normally the slowness in collecting cash from credit sales. Your profit and loss statement may show your gross sales, but your cash flow statement will reveal how much of it was converted to cash. Pull or print your accounts receivable detail and look to see who owes you, and how long it's been owed to you. Starting with the higher balances, call your customers to get the cash in. To monitor cash collections and availability, run a Receivables Turnover ratio and current ratio. The receivables turnover ratio tells how many times it's taking you to collect your cash from credit sales. Most businesses run this ratio annually, but you can monitor this monthly by taking your total credit sales for the month and dividing it by your uncollected credit sales (accounts receivable) for that month. If this ratio is high (4 and up), then you are efficient at your collections, but if it is low (1 to 3) then it means you need to work on getting credit sales converted to cash quicker. The Current Ratio which is also called liquidity ratio, or the working capital ratio, tells you if you have enough cash to keep your business going monthly. Sometimes looking at the dollar figures is just not enough, you want to know what the numbers mean. To calculated the current ratio, add up your cash and cash equivalents, then divide it by your total monthly liabilities. A ratio of greater than one means that you have more than enough to cover your monthly expenses. For more on ratios revisit chapter three.

Your operating profits are declining.

Low operating profits could result because you are not generating enough sales, you are mismanaging funds, or because you reduced your marketing efforts. What you may want to do to turn things around is check your sales goals and marketing plan to ensure that you and your team are following through with the plans. If you do not have a sales goal in place then that's the first thing you want to get done, because without your sales plan in place you are trying to generate revenue without any sense of direction. Once you get your sales plan in place you will need to formulate a marketing plan to help you reach your sales goals. It's much easier to break up your sales goals into monthly targets and assess them every quarter, that's every three months. Chapter three offers marketing plan insights and chapter seven offers ideas about how to generate revenues. If you are mismanaging funds, then implement the cash management ideas mentioned in this chapter.

Your business debt exceeds your equity.

When you look at your balance sheet, your assets should equal the sum of your business debts plus the investment that you put into the business. Assets are acquired and business is funded in one of two ways, (a) either by debt—a loan you took from the bank or family, or (b) money that you or an investor put into the business. Your true equity is revealed when all your debts are paid off. If your debts are more than your equity this means that, if all your debts were due today you may be put into a situation where you have to file bankruptcy. To turn things around, retain more profits in the business, restrict cash and transfer it to a savings account or invest the money into something that will give you a greater return on your money. You can also work-out a plan to reduce or eliminate your debt. Debt repayment is discussed in chapter nine. You can use the debt to equity ratio shown in chapter three to assess your ability to repay your debts. As a general rule, your equity should be at least one and a half times more than your debt.

You have one major client.

When your business is new it is wonderful to get that one big client, but don't get comfortable with that. Think of it as an opportunity to work on getting in new clients or customers without feeling the pressure and stress of getting revenue into the business. This is important because if your one big client decides to do business elsewhere you will be impacted significantly by the change. Avoid relying on one or even two major clients and work towards building your business and having multiple streams of income.

High turnover of staff or contract workers.

If you are not paying your staff on time, setting unrealistic expectations, and treating your staff with disrespect you may have a very hard time retaining good help. When your staff feels unappreciated or disrespected it may show up in how they treat your customers or in the quality of their work. Sometimes, a staff may even quit in the middle of a major project or busy time, this can cause major interruptions in your business. Communicate with your team, pay them well and value their input so that they will help you grow your business as if it were their own. Too much turnover of staff slows down production and can hurt customer service. You can start fixing this issue by calling a team meeting and getting feedback from you team about how things can be improved.

Declining customers.

If you are experiencing a decline in the amount of customers you have, you may not be offering quality service or keeping your customers engaged. Unhappy customers many eventually lead to reduced sales and without revenue you may run into financial hardship. Make sure you are listening to your customers and identifying their needs, by doing so you can work towards customizing services or even products to meet those needs. Ensure that you and your staff continue to offer your customers your best. Connect with your customers and keep them interested through marketing, surveys, customer appreciation events, gifts, discounts, emails or thank you cards—depending on your industry.

Expanding too fast.

Rapid expansion may result in cash reduction, which can lead to further financial problems. The growth of your revenues should be the proof that you should consider expanding, not because you think you should expand or because someone points out an opportunity. You are looking at the demand or need for your services or products in an area, if there's a market for it. Don't spread yourself too thin, put together a plan and allow things to evolve in the course of time as you get your finances in order. If you have already begun to spread yourself too thin and you are running short on cash, revisit the suggestions for generating revenues and put together a plan to keep you profitable.

Behind on Rent.

Sometimes you may not notice a decline in revenues or in your customers, but you are struggling to manage your cash and behind on your rent payments. A lock-out or an eviction from your place of business can result in business interruption and the loss of revenue. Make it a priority to manage your funds wisely, implement effective cash management strategies to keep your business growing. See chapter three for commercial lease options. When your rent becomes late your landlord will usually assess a late fee for the late rent plus additional charges for each day late possibly. You need to know what the terms and conditions are if you fall behind on your rent payment, like how much time you have before you are locked out and what steps you need to take. Some business owners do not take the time to go over all the fine details of the lease agreement—at minimum have a lawyer review your lease agreement for you. Before a tenant is locked-out the landlord or property manager will issue a notice. Once a tenant is locked-out, they will no longer have access to their business space and whatever items are in the space. If the rent plus the late charges and attorney fees are not paid by a certain due date, then the formal eviction procedure will follow. This is when things usually get really ugly, because a tenant could be legally responsible for the entire rent for the remaining duration of the lease contract. So, this is no joking matter, you must understand what's in your lease agreement. If you are currently in this situation, you are going to have to be proactive with finding a solution to keep you in your space. Get your attorney to negotiate an alternative to keep you in the property, but you have to do this early because if the answer is "no" you are going to have to move on to plan number two. Communicate with the property managers, sometimes they can work out a solution to help you stay in your space. This is more likely if you are a good tenant, and they know how challenging it can be to find good tenants. You may also try to see if the landlord will terminate your lease early. You will probably be asked to pay a certain amount of the lease, but your credit will not be impacted and you will be free from incurring further debt.

Trickling Revenues.

If have been in business for at least seven months and you have no to very low sales, then you may want to check your business model. This could mean that there's something wrong with your marketing channels or the value that you are communicating to your customers. This is common as every business owner at some point has tried to figure out what formula will work best for their business. Refer back to chapter three on what is required to make your business work. Without cash flow coming into your business it will be very hard to keep your business operating.

LESSONS IN BUSINESS

9

BUILDING WEALTH

"The plans of the diligent lead to profit as surely as haste leads to poverty... The wisdom of the prudent is to give thought to their ways."

~ A PROVERB OF SOLOMON

During the introductory session of an advance accounting class that I was teaching at the University of Phoenix, a student of mine noted with boldness and confidence that she wanted to be "Independently wealthy". I had never met anyone till that day who openly admitted such a desire—it was refreshing. That's because some people snub at the idea of being rich, but the truth is that most people in the world wish they were wealthy. In their minds they think of all the problems they could solve, perhaps eliminate world poverty, find a cure for illnesses, support various missionary causes, build quality shelters for orphan children, establish schools in remote villages—well some people think of these. Others think of the luxury car they would buy, the house they would purchase, the vacations they would take, how many shopping sprees they would go on or how they would change their own lives for the better. Money does not solve everything, but it is one of the main reasons so many people are stressed in the world. The constant shortage of it keeps people from focusing on the more important matters in life, because their focus is always on how to get more money so they can advance their social class or solve their problems. That day in class my student's out spoken talk of wealth started a whole new conversation, and now the rest of the class wanted to know how people become wealthy. If you ask someone what being wealthy means to them it would be different for everyone. People who come from extreme poverty might say that attaining a middle class status would be a dream come true, while a person who grew up middle class might view wealthy as being a part of the upper class. But what is true wealth? It depends who you ask. However, by definition wealth is having a lot of money and possessions according to the Merriam-Webster's dictionary. But having lots of money and possessions is not what most self- employed people are after; most people went into business for financial independence.

Financial independence means having enough money to live on without having to work actively for your basic living needs. Basic living needs are food, water, shelter, clothing, access to healthcare, and perhaps education and transportation also. But self-employed people do work actively for their basic living needs, so what's the point of being self-employed? At first, a glimpse of this definition appears to be no different from being employed, except that self-employed individuals have to build a brand from scratch, many of them can't afford health insurance and work more hours than when they were employed. But if you assess what self-employment really is, you will see that the state of being self-employed offers independence. It gives one the opportunity to chart their own course; and this is why discipline is a very important trait to have in order to be successful in business. In addition, for many people who were not born into wealthy families, self-employment is a gateway to build wealth. However, it would be wise to work towards achieving financial independence and perhaps over time wealth may follow. One should never see wealth as the ultimate goal in life, after all money is simply a means to an end. The question you should ask yourself is—why am I doing what I am doing? What results am I trying to achieve? There is no right or wrong answer to this question, but as long as you can answer it truthfully, then you will have a better clarification of which direction you should take for your financial wellbeing. As time goes on the economy changes, people go through life cycles, and situations happen in life. As such, to ensure your wellbeing and that of your family for generations to come, you must learn to accumulate, manage and grow your income wisely.

BE PRUDENT

Most people work so hard, but only a few people ever achieve their financial goals. Some solopreneurs begin to generate a lot of revenues and get stuck trying to control their business cost. Others manage to make it to profits but never get to wealth because as soon as the money starts flowing in they are off buying depreciating items like luxury cars, or assets that do not generate future income. Some even venture into buying luxury homes that they will not be able to maintain with peace of mind. There's nothing wrong with buying luxury items, but if you are trying to build wealth or at least achieve financial independence you cannot spend money frivolously. The opportunity that you have now as a self-employed person should be treated with gratitude and carried on with wisdom. There are no short cuts, you will have to put in the time and effort to achieve results and you will have to exercise self-control and discipline in order to escape the urge to spend impulsively. Most self-employed people are not from wealthy families, many were fired or laid-off from their jobs, could not find work or stepped out by faith in search of financial independence and work-life balance. With this in mind we can perhaps safely assume that many self- employed people are starting off with very little, zero or negative Net Worth. This means that there's a big gap between their current financial standing and financial independence. Below is a chart obtained from the 2012 U.S. Census Bureau showing the sales revenue of self-employed persons also referred to as nonemployer. Take a moment to review the nonemployer gross receipts chart in table 9.1.

Over 89 percent of self-employed people make less than $100,000 in gross receipts, which means that the net earnings are far less after expenses and taxes are paid. An analysis of this information when matched against household incomes by social classes (see table 9.2) would show that 89 percent of self- employed business owners could be either in the middle class or still at the working class level.

Table 9.1

Geographic area name	2012 NAICS code	Meaning of 2012 NAICS code	Meaning of Receipt size of establishments	Year	Number of nonemployer establishments
United States	00	Total for all sectors	All establishments	2012	22,735,915
United States	00	Total for all sectors	Establishments with sales or receipts less than $5,000	2012	5,519,673
United States	00	Total for all sectors	Establishments with sales or receipts of $5,000 to $9,999	2012	3,767,416
United States	00	Total for all sectors	Establishments with sales or receipts of $10,000 to $24,999	2012	5,692,845
United States	00	Total for all sectors	Establishments with sales or receipts of $25,000 to $49,999	2012	3,094,407
United States	00	Total for all sectors	Establishments with sales or receipts of $50,000 to $99,999	2012	2,212,148
United States	00	Total for all sectors	Establishments with sales or receipts of $100,000 to $249,999	2012	1,682,694
United States	00	Total for all sectors	Establishments with sales or receipts of $250,000 to $499,999	2012	513,137
United States	00	Total for all sectors	Establishments with sales or receipts of $500,000 to $999,999	2012	221,815
United States	00	Total for all sectors	Establishments with sales or receipts of $1,000,000 to $2,499,999	2012	29,494
United States	00	Total for all sectors	Establishments with sales or receipts of $2,500,000 to $4,999,999	2012	1,900
United States	00	Total for all sectors	Establishments with sales or receipts of $5,000,000 or more	2012	386

Nonemployer Statistics is an annual series that provides subnational economic data for businesses that have no paid employees and are subject to federal income tax. The data consist of the number of businesses and total receipts by industry. Most nonemployers are self-employed individuals operating unincorporated businesses (known as sole proprietorships), which may or may not be the owner's principal source of income.

This implies that only about 11percent of self-employed business owners actually advance towards becoming financially independent. Which brings us back to a question asked in the introductory of this book; why are so many people broke? In this section we will focus our attention on what influences a person's ability to achieve *Financial Independence* since *Wealth* is just the abundance of money and possessions. Educated with this information, you can begin to work your way out of financial instability and confidently build a secure financial future.

Table 9.2 Household Incomes by Class

SOCIAL CLASS	INCOME RANGE	EDUCATION LEVELS	WHAT THEY DO
The Upper Class	$350,000+	Ivy league education	Executives, CEOs, Business Owners
The Upper Middle Class	$80,000 - $300,000	Graduate Degree	Corporate Professionals and Nonemployer Professionals
The Middle Class	$35,000 - $75,000	Bachelor's Degree	Managers
Working Class	$15,000 - $30,000	Some College	Blue Collar & Services
The Lower Class	$0 - $10,000	High School	Part time, Clerical & Government Assistance

UNDERSTANDING NET WORTH

Generally, the net worth of most upper class people is over $1 million, but table shows that the upper class income is about $350,000 or more, so how do they have over $1 million in net worth? Net Worth is the financial standing of an individual after all liabilities have been paid or if they were to be paid. For example, if an individual has assets of $410,000 and liabilities of $240,000, their net worth would be $170,000 as shown in figure 9.1.

Assets		
Cash and Securities	$ 80,000	
Personal Residence	$ 300,000	
Automobiles	$ 30,000	
Total Assets		$ 410,000
Liabilities		
Mortgage	$ 220,000	
Auto Loans	$ 20,000	
Total Liabilities		$ 240,000
Personal Net Worth		$ 170,000

Figure 9.1

Net Worth however is never fixed; it's just a snapshot of person's worth at a particular moment in time just like the balance sheet of a business. A person's net worth can change in just the twinkle of an eye. Using figure 9.1 let's examine how this can happen. What if the market value of the listed securities declined? Then the net worth shown would also decline. Similarly, if the cost of living increased due to the weakening of the buying power of currency (inflation), then the available cash would not be enough to cover current living expenses as before. Also, assuming there was no income being generated and more cash was needed, the personal residence and automobiles would have to be sold in order to get the cash to pay off debts. But since these could go down in value, by the time it is sold , it may not be enough to cover the debt owed; this is how net worth can change at any moment. The debt however will continue to accrue interest on top of the remaining principle balance. Now, since this person has no more income from self-employment perhaps due to illness or bad economic times, how do they pay off the debt with these declining asset values? Inflation creeps in every year which means that cost of living also rises every year. How can a person keep up their lifestyle with such choices and inevitable life events? This is why so many people in the middle class fall closer to the poverty line as the years go by if they do not change their financial behaviors. This is why high income does not guarantee financial freedom. Adopting sound financial principles is what will get you through those inevitable economic events and life changes. It is what those who have held generations of financial stability have used for years.

In order for you to increase your net worth you must collect more assets than liabilities, but it must be the right assets. Assets like your primary residence and cars should not be your primary focus. These assets actually come with added costs, such as property taxes and maintenance, which deplete your cash reserves and they do not generate income for you. The automobiles particularly always depreciates in value, and a home can decline in value, but it can also increase significantly in value. Usually homes in elite and well-kept neighborhoods have a stronger chance of holding their value over time. The mistake people make is they figure that their home will significantly go up enough in value to provide income for their retirement years. How can that happen when you do not know for certain what it will be worth in the future, or what the cost of living will be at that time, and even if you happen to borrow money from a bank against the equity in your home, how do you plan to pay back the bank in your retirement? Retirement does imply that you are not actively working for a living any longer, so where will you get money to support your basic living needs? The lessons to follow will give you insights for attaining financial independence. They have been proven through generations to help people defeat financial struggles and place them on the pathway to true financial independence.

LESSONS IN ACHIEVING FINANCIAL INDEPENDENCE

Lesson One

Money is a necessity, so increase your ability to earn it.

Money is a medium of exchange, in the past barter, gold, and other commodities were used as mediums of exchange. There are still a few self- employed people who use the barter method to receive and provide services, but this method does not offer the ability to transfer the bartered item to acquire other goods and services more openly. As such, money remains the primary way to get the things we want and need, therefore money is a necessity. It is your means of support and without it, getting through the affairs of life can be a struggle. So, you need enough money to support yourself and that of your family, but no one is going to give it to you. As a self-employed individual the only way you are going to get money is to work for it, as the proverb says *"All hard work brings a profit, but mere talk leads only to poverty."* Work your business and look for opportunities to multiply your revenue sources. Focus on your area of expertise, but expand your sources of business income within your focus area. It is also important for you to know what other types of income exist aside from self-employment income, this way you will be aware of other options that may be more suitable for your life situation.

There are three fundamental income types, Earned Income, Portfolio Income, and Passive Income. As a self-employed individual you are earning your money, which means that you must do the work in order to get money. This is why the method of obtaining the income is termed *earned*; salaries, tips, wages and commission are also examples of earned income. Some people also refer to it as *active income* since you must actively be involved in the process of acquiring the money. However, when it comes to financial planning for the long term, especially for the years in which you will not be as active in your business, you will need a way to bring in income without having to put in the long work hours.

A good and proven way to ensure income in future years is to transition some of your money into passive and portfolio Income. Portfolio income is a way of generating money without you personally having to work for it. Portfolio income is money obtained from capital gains, dividends, royalties, interest, and other forms of investment, but it is not passive income even though several people have confused the two types. Passive income is money obtained from a business, such as a partnership in which you are not actively involved in the management of the business but you have partial ownership in it, or rental property that you own. Both portfolio and passive income do not require you to actively do the work in order to get the money, but both normally require monetary investment in order to generate income from them.

Lesson Two

Keep more of your earnings
by spending less than what you receive.

There really is no other way to retain money once it's is in your possession other than to keep what you received. But unfortunately you can't hold on to all of it because you have bills to pay and other needs that cost money. What you can do is to spend less of it by paying careful attention to where you are transferring your money to and why. You must understand that when you spend money you are actually transferring it to another entity be it a person or business, in exchange for something else. For example, if you were hungry but you have no food to eat, you will probably go to the grocery store to buy food or eat out at a restaurant. Well, the very act of you buying the food says that you are willing to exchange or give up your money to get the food items. Once you buy it, you have transferred money out from your bank to someone else's. Likewise when your customers or clients buy your products or pay for your services they are transferring their money to you in exchange for what you have to offer. If most people thought about their spending in this manner, they would probably not have purchased many of the things they purchased in the past. Figure 9.2 is an illustration of how money flows from one entity to the next.

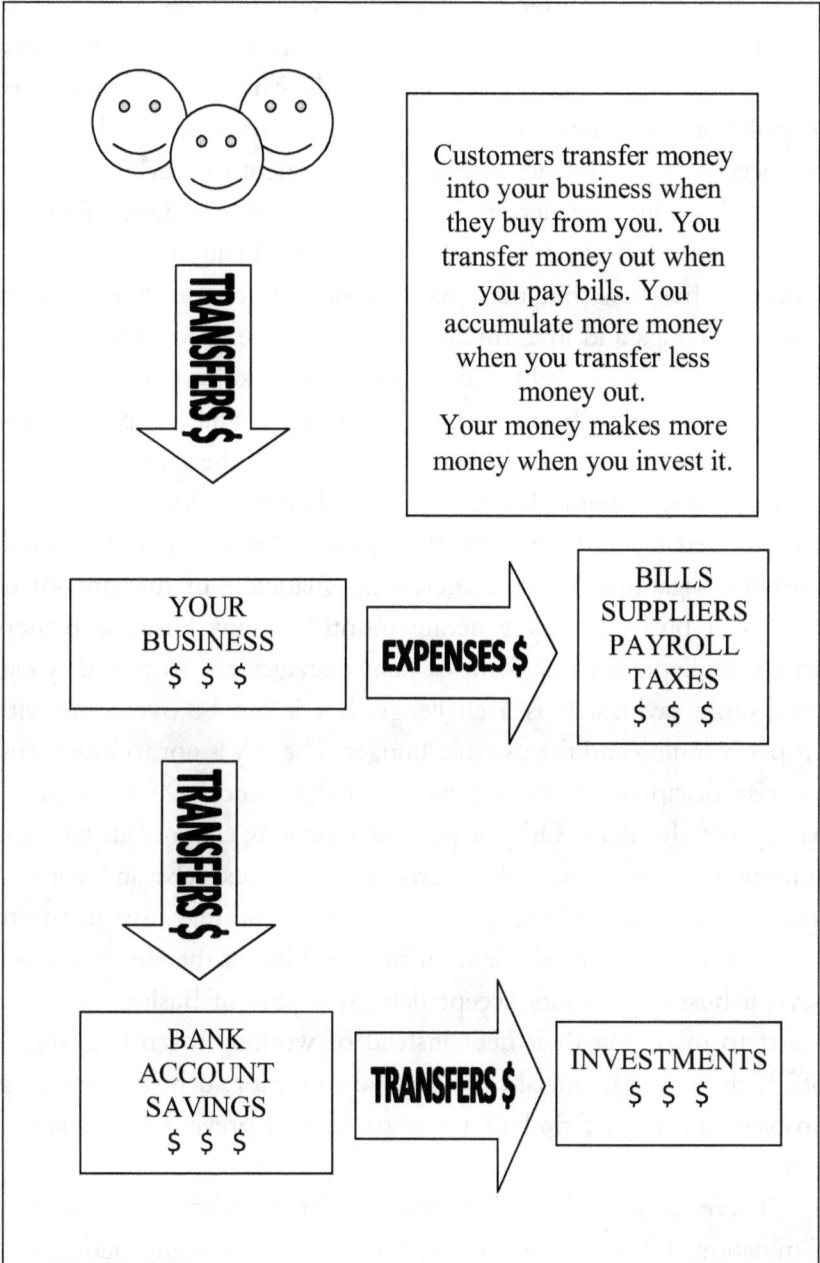

Customers transfer money into your business when they buy from you. You transfer money out when you pay bills. You accumulate more money when you transfer less money out.
Your money makes more money when you invest it.

TRANSFERS $

YOUR BUSINESS $ $ $

EXPENSES $

BILLS SUPPLIERS PAYROLL TAXES $ $ $

TRANSFERS $

BANK ACCOUNT SAVINGS $ $ $

TRANSFERS $

INVESTMENTS $ $ $

Figure 9.2

One of the main obstacles preventing many business owners from saving money is debt that was incurred before the formation of their business. Many self-employed individuals carry large balances of school loans, car notes, medical bills and other types of debts that can become burdensome. Paying down the debt can even appear to be a big inconvenience when trying to achieve financial independence. A business owner in this situation may have a profitable business, but they may not be able to use their earnings towards savings and investments because of the need to payoff that debt. The bigger the debt, the longer it may take to pay it off, even for a very profitable business. Debts may take a while to pay because of the need to use the available cash to cover all the various demands of the business. Some business owners become very overwhelmed and stressed trying to balance their personal needs, past debts and current obligations. Because there's no guarantee of the amount of revenue a business may generate monthly, many business owners usually implement some form of debt management so that they can have some savings. It is a challenge, but it can be overcome with proper planning and the use of a budget. The key is not to lose focus, exercise discipline in sticking with a budget, and have a system of paying off the debt. Once a particular debt is eliminated, take the amount that was allocated towards the pervious debt and apply it towards the other debt to pay it off faster. You may also decide to stick with your debt elimination plan and invest the freed up cash. Several business owners accept debt as a part of business life and resort to managing their debt instead of working towards paying it off. If there is a financial need they take on more debt to solve their problem, instead of finding a way to fix and prevent that financial issue.

There is a difference between debt management and debt elimination. Debt management is the act of controlling debt, many people associate debt management with companies that negotiate with creditors on behalf of the debtors for lower interest rates, to reduce the liability, and allocate the monthly payments to help eliminate the debt. But anyone can manage their own debt if they make it a priority and work with a budget. People that outsource the management of their debt to a debt management company do so because they lack the discipline or time to do so, but at least they are doing something about it and that's great. Debt elimination requires a different mindset and even more discipline. With debt elimination, the goal is not to manage the money overtime with monthly payments, but to get rid of it using a strategic approach. Most people that choose debt management as a way to administer their debt are usually concerned with the preservation or enhancement of their credit scores, while people who choose debt elimination are more concerned with a permanent solution that will set them free from the bondage of debt and offer them the ability to have total control over their money and how they use it. Debt elimination could result in lower credit scores depending on what strategy is used, but at least the end result is freedom from debt. Regardless of the choice to eliminate debt or manage it, the point is to work out your affairs wisely so that you will be in a position to keep more of the money transferred to you for use towards achieving financial freedom.

A few words about repaying debt

It would be great to just pay off debt as money comes into the business, and this is very possible for many people. However, there are some people who just do not have the ability to do so, and as such they need a structured system to tackle their debts. Drowning in debt is a horrible feeling, and there are many people who have been perplexed by how quickly things can get out of hand—but there is hope. If you dread going to the mail box, answering your phone, and tired of shifting money around weekly just so you can make ends meet, you are not alone. Before choosing a method to handle your debt, consider your unique situation. Every person's financial situation is different and every business does not make the same revenues monthly. For example, the snowball method which is emphasized by personal finance expert Dave Ramsey, may not work for you in its original form if you are not even in a position to make minimum payments.

If you are trying to eliminate your debts with limited resources you may have to get on a strict savings plan to put away some money first for about three to six months before starting your debt repayment plan. This means that you will have to put a hold on paying any person or company so that you can get yourself together; and this means that your credit may go bad, so getting a loan is out of the question. But getting into further debt should not be on your agenda unless you are investing into an immediate cash flow producing activity that will produce enough income for you to pay off the existing debt plus the new one. Further, if you are in a debt crisis, most lenders will not lend to you anyway, because you probably defaulted on the previous debt. If you are at such a place at this time in your life, being in debt does not make you a horrible person—everyone makes mistakes and unexpected events occur. The main thing is how you handle things moving forward. Even if it makes you feel sick, contact the person or company you owe and explain your situation and apologize (sincerely), and get moving with your debt repayment plan. Take no calls from annoying debt collectors to preserve your focus and confidence, focus on working your business to generate income—it takes money to pay off the debt. So, focus on bringing in money, cover only your essential operating expenses and basic living needs, but put away as much as you can to get a good start on your repayment plan. Deny yourself every delight and scale down to the basics, downsize if you must, sell whatever you don't need to get in some money, and add the income to your savings. It takes radical focus to overcome major challenges, as well as time. If you owe people money, some may never speak with you again, some may remind you of your low moments whenever possible, but rise above the noise and focus on your goals—make it a hard lesson learned and one never to be repeated. Work hard to succeed; you will come overcome this situation.

CONSIDER THIS...

Bill collectors only want one thing—their money! Once you've made arrangements to pay off a debt, there is no need to continue answering annoying phone calls. Focus your time and energy on getting money to pay the debt off. In addition, if you are not able to meet your payment deadline notify them and keep focus on getting the bill paid rather than entertaining distracting collection calls.

DEBT ELIMINATION TECHNIQUES

1. Document every debt you owe and list them in order from the smallest balance to the highest balance. This is debt—your loans, credit cards, etc., not your operating expenses that are billed to your business monthly.

2. Next to each debt list the minimum payment you are require to pay, if it changes monthly estimate an average.

3. Review your operating budget to determine the maximum amount you can afford to pay each month toward your total debt.

4. Add up all your minimum payments and subtract that figure from the maximum amount you can afford to pay each month.

5. If you have more than enough, then make your minimum payments and apply the difference to the smallest debt. Once the smallest debt is paid off, take the amount you were paying towards the smallest debt and apply it towards the next smallest debt.

6. Continue this until all your debts are paid off.

Alternative Option

If you don't have enough to pay on all your minimum payments, pay no one and save up as much money as possible for three to six months, then, do one of the following:

1. Contact your creditors to see if they can reduce your minimum payments, if they can, repeat step four above and continue with the repayment plan. If you still can't meet your minimum payments or your creditors will not revise your payments, then starting with the smallest debt, determine how many payments it will take you to pay off the smallest debt and still meet your operating and personal expenses, continue with option two below.

2. Determined how many installment payments it will take to pay off each debt, this determination should be based on the budgeted maximum amount you can afford to apply each month toward your total debt. Then, apply your determined installment payments to the smallest debt, and get that paid. Once the smallest debt is paid off, take the amount you were paying towards the smallest debt and apply it towards the next smallest debt. Continue this until all your debts are paid off.

DEBT MANAGEMENT TECHNIQUES

1. Document every debt you owe and list them in order from the least to the greatest balance.

2. Next to each debt list the minimum payment you are currently require to pay, if it changes monthly estimate an average.

3. Review your operating budget to determine the maximum amount you can afford to pay each month toward your total debt.

4. Add up all your minimum payments and subtract that figure from the maximum amount you can afford to pay each month.

5. If you have more than enough to cover your minimum payments, take the excess and set it aside as savings for future investments. Once you have saved enough to invest in an income producing asset, put your money to work for you.

6. Maintain your monthly payments timely until you get to a point where you can pay them off.

Alternative Option

1. Contact your creditors to see if they can reduce your monthly payment amount and arrange a more suitable payment option. This will give you some freed-up cash to apply towards income producing activities and to grow your business.

2. If you are behind on your debt obligation, ask your creditors if they can arrange an alternative payment plan for you, and start making payments on the agreed upon date. Keep in mind that you need money to pay off debt, so work your business.

Borrowing more money to pay off debts may get you further in debt; remember, you have interest payments that accrue monthly—just the opposite of compounding interest on an investment. Making little payments monthly will result in a much longer time frame to pay off your debt, accomplishing very little. So the purpose of debt management is to create an opportunity for you to have money to reinvest into your business and generate more money. Two to five years in business, if operated wisely, may very well get you enough money to pay off all your debts in less time. So invest in your business and work your business to get results.

Lesson Three

Invest your business profits
and let your money work for you.

Previously it was noted that the net worth of most upper class people is over $1 million, but figure 9.2 shows that the upper class income is about $350,000 or more, so how do they have over $1 million in net worth? Well, you have probably heard people say "the rich get richer", the reason the rich get richer is because they learned how to make their money grow. Not all wealthy people were born into wealthy families, many of them started in a similar situation like yours and some even came from extreme poverty. At some point in their life someone shared with them the financial principles and they acted upon the advice. As time passed they began to see the fruits of their efforts manifest and they continued to stick with those principles. One of those principles was to let their money work for them. The very act of letting your money work for you means investing your money in something that will create more money for you. So instead of your excess money sitting in a non-interest bearing checking account, you should put that money to work no matter how small you may think the amount is. The work that is taking place is the production of dividends, interest, equity or any other return on an investment. The proceeds from the investments are then reinvested to reproduce further. So, in other words, you have labored for the money, but you can take the money earned and invest it so that it will produce more money for you.

What can you invest in to let your money work for you? In lesson one you learned about the three fundamental income types,

Earned Income, Portfolio Income, and Passive Income. Being self-employed you have already taken on a form of investment by starting a business. You have taken money that you saved up and invested that into a small business, and when your business generates a profit you take the money and reinvest it back into your business. As your business begins to grow, you should employ people and integrate a system where your business begins to depend less on you having to be present at all times in order for it to function. Once your business starts to function without requiring your presence, the profits you get from it will be considered passive income from a business ownership. This passive income from business equity is one way the upper class makes their money. Many of them own partnership interest and ownership shares in various entities, as these businesses flourish they harvest their share of profits and reinvest them again. Another approach used is establishing a portfolio with some assets that employ the effect of compound interest. Compound interest is interest that has been earned on the principal amount of a loan (you are the lender), or a bank deposit and the interest is added to the principal amount and it also earns interest. The actual compounding is the interest earning interest throughout the loan term or as long as the deposit continues to accrue interest. Figure 9.3 shows an example of compounding interest. Bonds, private loans, and bank deposits, are a few types of assets that compound interest. It is said that Albert Einstein, theoretical physicist and 1921 Nobel Prize recipient known for his development of the general theory of relativity, once stated that compound interest is the greatest mathematical discovery of all time. Owning stock, real estate, bonds, and commodities are all examples of assets that offer you the opportunity to let your money make money for you; we will elaborate on these assets in lesson four.

Compound Interest Example One: One time savings deposit	
Initial Savings	$5,000
Years	10 years
Additional contributions	$0 per month
Rate of return	5%
Total amount you will have contributed	$5,000
Total interest	$3,235.12
Total at end of investment	$8,235.12

Figure 9.3(a)

Year	Additions	Interest	Balance
Start	$5,000.00		$5,000.00
1	$0	$255.81	$5,255.81
2	$0	$268.89	$5,524.70
3	$0	$282.67	$5,807.37
4	$0	$297.12	$6,104.49
5	$0	$312.34	$6,416.83
6	$0	$328.31	$6,745.14
7	$0	$345.10	$7,090.24
8	$0	$362.76	$7,453.00
9	$0	$381.29	$7,834.29
10	$0	$400.83	$8,235.12

Figure 9.3(b)

Figure 9.3 shows what the interest earnings will be on a one time deposit of $5,000 with interest that compounds. The interest is compounded monthly at an annual interest rate of 5% for ten years. As shown, no additional monthly deposits were add throughout the ten year period.

Figure 9.4 shows the effect of compounding interest when the same five thousand dollars is deposited into an investment earning a monthly compounding annual interest of 5%, and has monthly deposits of $400 added to it. Just imagine how much a working adolescent would have for college if their earnings were put into some type of investment compounding interest overtime. Even if a student goes to school on a full scholarship, imagine what a difference it would make after graduation.

Compound Interest Example Two: Monthly savings deposit	
Initial savings	$5,000
Years	10 years
Monthly additions to savings	$400 per month
Annual Interest	5%
Sum of additions to savings	$53,000
Total interest received	$17,606.81
Total savings at ten years	$70,606.81

Figure 9.4(a)

Year	Additions	Interest	Balance
Year	$5,000.00		$5,000.00
1	$4,800.00	$387.82	$10,187.82
2	$4,800.00	$653.24	$15,641.06
3	$4,800.00	$932.25	$21,373.31
4	$4,800.00	$1,225.51	$27,398.82
5	$4,800.00	$1,533.79	$33,732.61
6	$4,800.00	$1,857.84	$40,390.45
7	$4,800.00	$2,198.45	$47,388.90
8	$4,800.00	$2,556.52	$54,745.42
9	$4,800.00	$2,932.88	$62,478.30
10	$4,800.00	$3,328.51	$70,606.81

Figure 9.4(b)

Lesson Four

Plan for future years' Income

Previously, you learned about generating revenue for your business, and you also learned about the importance of having various revenues streams. Well, the monthly revenues being generated from the different sources is actually an inflow of cash coming into your business. We discussed the term cash flow previously, it is the transfer of money into or out of your business. It could also be the transfer of money into or out of your personal financial depository. To help you maintain a consistent inflow of money to keep up your living standards and pay for obligations for years to come, it is important for you to have a constant inflow of cash that will not depend on your constant physical involvement. Many of the options available for investing your business profits to let your money work for you are also good producers of cash inflows.

For example, interest earned on a deposit account can be transferred into your bank account monthly or quarterly, but doing so will reduce the benefits obtained from compounding interest. Likewise you can also collect dividends when paid instead of reinvesting it to acquire more shares of stock, and you can decide to have your share of business profits paid to you monthly or quarterly as well.

Securing passive and portfolio income is essential in planning for future year's income. It is also important in order to maintain financial independence for several reasons, the most important is for when you can no longer actively earn your income it will give you the ability to maintain your standard of living. You don't want to be in a situation where you suddenly have to figure out how to stretch your lump sum of savings or retirement funds over a long period of time. You also don't want to be forced to work, especially during your senior years because you have to in order to meet basic living needs. In addition, because inflation will cause the cost of living to increase you want to be in a position where if you have to help with your child's education, cover the cost of health care, or care for your aging parents, offering such support will not restrict your quality of living. You should also give yourself permission to enjoy life, to relax and focus on more meaningful causes, rather than spending your life working and paying bills. After all one's entire life should not consist in the accumulation of things or just working to pay off debt. Generally there are two ways to acquire passive and portfolio income. You can either invest large sums of money that you inherited or take your earnings saved up over the years and invest in assets that will generate income; or if you have no money or limited funds you can use your skills and experience to acquire or create assets that will give you revenue streams. Table 9.3 shows a sampling of assets that generate income.

Table 9.3

PASSIVE AND PORTFOLIO IN COME USING MONEY	PASSIVE AND PORTFOLIO INCOME USING SKILLS AND EXPERIENCE
<ul><li>Rental income from leased residential and commercial property.</li><li>Dividends income from stocks.</li><li>Interest income from bank deposits and bonds.</li><li>Profits from business equity.</li><li>Interest income from private loans.</li><li>Profits from your business establishment.</li><li>Earnings from commodities like oil, barley, coco beans, gold and silver.</li></ul>	<ul><li>Profits from an Internet business or an established business with employees.</li><li>Royalties from copy rights like books, training materials, music CD & DVDs, movies and other published works.</li><li>Royalties from patented work like licensing for inventions and designs.</li><li>Dividends from stock ownership acquired from invested time and knowledge in a business.</li><li>Business equity obtained through invested time and knowledge in a business.</li><li>Recurring commissions from insurance sales and multi-level marketing.</li><li>Licensing fees from trademarks on created brands.</li></ul>

Lesson Five

Protect your Assets

Imagine being reacquainted with an old friend who's now in real estate at a business networking event. You and your real estate friend begin a conversation which turns out to be very engaging and meaningful. During the conversation you find out that there is a four unit apartment building selling below the fair market value—it's in foreclosure. You have never bought real estate before, but you have always wanted to start a real property portfolio and you believe that this is your chance to start. You begin to inquire about the price and the possibility of buying the property, your real estate friend ask you to come by the office the next day to sign a contract because the property will be off the market, predictably in a day and you'll miss out on a great opportunity. You ask for the property address and look it up online to see where it's located and what it looks like. It's in a good neighborhood and close to shops and public transportation; "it will be an excellent rental" you tell yourself. The following day you take a joyful trip to the office to sign the contract; your real estate friend tells you that because it's a foreclosure the sale must be finalized in five days and the funds must be remitted with a cashier's check or electronically. You are going to be out on a business trip for three days, so you don't have time to shop for a lender. Upon your return you decide to have the funds transferred electronically for the closing, it's a little rushed, but you rationalized that at least you got a great property for a great price. Two months later you get two letters, one from the school district that a lien has been place on your property for back taxes, and it's up for auction if you don't pay up, and the other from a neighboring city for the same thing. You remember checking with the county tax office and all taxes were paid up to date. So confused, you decide to call the property tax office and they tell you that because of where the property is located you have to pay property tax to two cities and that the previous owner had a disability and homestead exemption (words that you have no clue as to what it means), but the school district prorates it differently. You contact the school district and they confirm two years property taxes owed plus penalties and interest. In addition, one of your tenant calls confirming if this is the new management office and when you are planning to resolve the pest issue and the leaking roof.

Not a great way to start your real estate investment venture. Being a knowledgeable investor is a crucial part of attaining financial independence. If you have an interest in acquiring certain assets that you are unfamiliar with take time to learn about them, and if you don't understand something ask for clarification. But don't limit your learning to only the exciting aspects of it; study both the upsides and downsides of investing in the various assets that are of interest to you. Sometimes, people get so excited about being able to take advantage of a great opportunity, that they neglect to do the basic due diligence and eventually find out that it was not as good a deal as it appeared. Using the previous story, there were so many oversights, for one an inspector should have been hired to take a look at the property, an appraisal and title search should have been ordered. The title search would have revealed any liens on the property and the inspector would have discovered the leaking roof and pest issue even in that short period of time. Also, be careful when doing business with friends and family; make sure that they are qualified in their field and never feel bad for not using a friend or family member who you do not feel comfortable working with. Ask the right questions to ensure that whoever you seek consultation from or employ to help you manage your assets has the knowledge and experience to do so. Sometimes, people feel compelled to give up-and-coming professionals an opportunity and that's okay, as long as you are sure that they have enough experience to do the work. Implementing strategies to help protect your assets from the impact of inflation is also very important. This is where investing in high yielding products come in handy or parking your money in assets that will increase in value as the cost of living also increases. It would be unpleasant to find out that money you had set aside today did not get you very far in five to ten years from now because you left the money idle in a non-interest bearing product. If your gut feeling is that an investment is unsafe or you don't feel comfortable with a transaction, then stay away from it or wait and do more research. There needs to be a balance between opportunity and prudence, because every opportunity is not a good opportunity. Attaining financial independence is like running a marathon not a sprint. Building a good financial portfolio a journey, it takes time, discipline, and diligence.

A Personal Financial Statement is a great way to keep track of your personal Assets and Liabilities. Just like you use your business financial statements to assess how well your business is doing and what needs to be done to improve it, you can use your personal financial statement to assess your personal net worth and see what you can do to improve your personal financial picture. This is a partial copy of a personal financial statement, a complete downloadable copy can be obtained from the U.S. Small Business Administration's website.

C.C VANNCE

OMB APPROVAL NO. 3245-0188
EXPIRATION DATE: 8/31/2011

PERSONAL FINANCIAL STATEMENT

U.S. SMALL BUSINESS ADMINISTRATION

As of _____ , _____

Complete this form for: (1) each proprietor, or (2) each limited partner who owns 20% or more interest and each general partner, or (3) each stockholder owning 20% or more of voting stock, or (4) any person or entity providing a guaranty on the loan.

Name	Business Phone
Residence Address	Residence Phone
City, State, & Zip Code	
Business Name of Applicant/Borrower	

ASSETS	(Omit Cents)	LIABILITIES	(Omit Cents)
Cash on hand & in Banks	$	Accounts Payable	$
Savings Accounts	$	Notes Payable to Banks and Others	$
IRA or Other Retirement Account	$	(Describe in Section 2)	
Accounts & Notes Receivable	$	Installment Account (Auto)	$
Life Insurance-Cash Surrender Value Only	$	Mo. Payments $	
(Complete Section 8)		Installment Account (Other)	$
Stocks and Bonds	$	Mo. Payments $	
(Describe in Section 3)		Loan on Life Insurance	$
Real Estate	$	Mortgages on Real Estate	$
(Describe in Section 4)		(Describe in Section 4)	
Automobile-Present Value	$	Unpaid Taxes	$
Other Personal Property	$	(Describe in Section 6)	
(Describe in Section 5)		Other Liabilities	$
Other Assets	$	(Describe in Section 7)	
(Describe in Section 5)		Total Liabilities	$
		Net Worth	$
Total	$	Total	$

Section 1. Source of Income		Contingent Liabilities	
Salary	$	As Endorser or Co-Maker	$
Net Investment Income	$	Legal Claims & Judgments	$
Real Estate Income	$	Provision for Federal Income Tax	$
Other Income (Describe below)*	$	Other Special Debt	$

Description of Other Income in Section 1.

*Alimony or child support payments need not be disclosed in "Other Income" unless it is desired to have such payments counted toward total income.

Section 2. Notes Payable to Banks and Others. (Use attachments if necessary. Each attachment must be identified as a part of this statement and signed.)

Name and Address of Noteholder(s)	Original Balance	Current Balance	Payment Amount	Frequency (monthly, etc.)	How Secured or Endorsed Type of Collateral

SBA Form 413 (10-08) **Previous Editions Obsolete**   (tumble)

This form was electronically produced by Elite Federal Forms, Inc.

PART FIVE

REACHING YOUR POTENTIAL

LESSONS IN BUSINESS

10

THE JOURNEY AHEAD

"Where focus goes energy flows."

~ TONY ROBBINS

Have you ever been in a hurry to get somewhere and suddenly you encountered traffic delays? How about traveling on holiday with family or friends and the weather turns ugly? Well, the journey to success is very similar to traveling to an exciting destination point. You pack your bags with all the things you think you need for the trip, enter your destination in the navigation system or secure your map so that you don't miss the way, and then unexpectedly something happens that causes a delay. It could be an accident, a road construction, weather condition, or simply rush hour that's causing the delays. But what do you do to get out of the traffic jams? Well, sometimes you take a detour, at times you just have to wait for the traffic to start moving again, and at some point the road eventually clears up and you are full speed ahead on to your destination point. There are moments when the road is just blocked off and you have to turn around and find another path to get to your destination. During this particular situation some people just give up and go back to where they came from instead of finding another route to their destination. Perhaps that destination point was not that important to them, and enduring the few uncomfortable moments of the trip was too much a price to pay for that particular destination. For example, if you were on your way to the mall and there was heavy traffic or the road was blocked because of construction, you might return home because it's not that important to you. But if you were going on vacation or to a very important meeting, then you would rather get there late, just as long as you get there and not miss the opportunity—because it's very important to you. Well, as you journey through the high and low moments of being self-employed, please know that what you are experiencing is not uncommon and you are not alone. Many individuals go through the ups and downs of being a business owner, but it is part of the growth process. As your business goes through the different stages of development you will also experience personal growth because you are maturing in your understanding of what being an entrepreneur is all about. You are transitioning from an employee mindset of following the rules and doing what's expected of you, to an entrepreneur state of mind in which you must think, create, and solve problems in order to achieve your goals.

Sometimes, you will encounter situations where the answers you are looking for are not obvious and opportunities you want fall through. You will have moments of utter frustration and times of great accomplishment. But no matter what situation arises remember your reason for venturing off into business and stay focus on your goals. Just as a seed is planted and eventually grows into a mature tree, so it is with a business. If you are diligent with your work, consistent in carrying out the behaviors and business principles essential to producing the right results, then your business will grow as well. You may not get the results you want at the very times you would like, but they will come. Many times you just have to seize your opportunity, but be very prudent and make sure that it is a good opportunity. Keep in mind that there are a lot of factors that can have an impact on the success of a business as discussed previously, the state of the economy, consumer behavior, the demand for a product or service and your ability to access the resources you need are just a few. You cannot control every situation, but you can use business principles as a guide to help you navigate your way to success.

DON'T LET EMOTIONS TAKE THE DRIVER SEAT

A decision based on emotions is no decision at all. This is very different from making a decision based on your instinct or as some may say gut feeling. Emotions in this instance refer o your current mood, such as anger, excitement, anxious, thankful, miserable or satisfied. For example, a father may feel uncomfortable around family for choosing a non-relative to manage the business, rather than his own son or daughter, even if the non-relative has the most experience and is the best choice to ensure the success of that business. The emotion here is a feeling of awkwardness or being uncomfortable for not choosing family. Another example is a business owner buying goods from a retailer with less quality products out of sheer obligation because of a favor to a friend, even when feeling skeptical about it; or firing a valued staff member out of anger because of a mistake that was made. Always, take time to assess the situation, even if it's just a moment. Now, while these examples of feelings may be adverse, making a decision based on positive feelings must also be weigh carefully as well. Excitement over possible opportunities, business deals, and invitations to participate in events, or join various organizations does not mean that it is the right choice for your business at the moment, or at all. If you make a decision based on your feelings you may end up regretting it or make a bad situation worse. If you have ever wrestled with decision making, below are a few steps that may help you.

Think of problems as bumps in the road. They might slow you down and even damage the car slightly, but it will not stop you from getting to your destination. Keep your focus on your goals and doing what is necessary to achieve them.

Decision Making: Choosing between two or more alternatives the best course of action for your business.

1. Recall your business goals and desired results.

2. Gather as much facts as possible about the choices. Even if you have to make a quick decision, gather as much information to allow you to make a well informed decision.

3. Determine which choice will put you in line with your business objectives. Compare the available choices and assess the advantages and disadvantages of each. Every decision should align in some way with your goals; it could be your long term or short term goals. For example, assume you are looking to generate more revenues in your business. You could have a short term goal and current focus of increasing sales of a specific product by a certain percentage within a six month time frame, and a long term goal of having total sales in the business at a specific amount in three years so that you can have the funds to

do other things that will help your business grow further. Since increasing sales is your current focus, then you should ensure that your business decisions will not prevent you from attaining your goals. Your decision should be based on existing knowledge and newly generate information about your choices.

4. Make a decision. This means selecting a choice from among the alternatives after you have thought things over.

5. Implement your decision by taking action. This could be as simple as picking up the phone to say "No thank you" or accepting a bid on a new project.

HOLD STEADY ON ROUGH ROADS

What happens when you get a flat tire on route to a destination? You don't just park the car on the road and forget about it, you change the tire and continue the journey. Neither do you turn away from bumpy roads, you simply exercise more control with the steering wheel and slow down to lessen the impact from the potholes and the chances of any damage to the car. Similarly, as you encounter problems or various challenges hold steady and don't let fear or worry divert you from your path. Challenges have a way of stretching people, imparting wisdom from the lessons learned to those who rise up to the challenge. Sometimes overcoming a challenge seems like "the right to advance"; sort of like in those games where you can only advance to the next level once you have passed the test and defeated, the enemy. When you are faced with a challenge, put into action the things you have learned about becoming successful.

One of the major causes of distraction for self-employed people is the stress brought on by the pressure to effectively manage personal finances. The battle to balance business and personal finances can be a daunting task and mentally exhausting. It is common for business owners to feel embarrassed about their financial struggles, even when nobody around them knows what happening. For some business owners their self- confidence diminishes, sometimes even blowing out the light of hope. All because of money problems in the home, a situation that can be solved with time, a plan and discipline. This problem arises because for some self- employed people who are not able to pay themselves a steady monthly income, they usually have to depend on the net profits of the business for income. Having sufficient funds to carry on daily operating activities is already a major issue for many small business owners, so if a business does generate a profit then the business owner may encounter financial hardship which can bring on tremendous stress. Business owners who operate under financial stress are more likely to make ill-advised decisions. They may also begin to experience feelings of discouragement towards their business, which can lead to a lack of focus. The main cause of financial stress is not knowing where the money will come from to pay the bills. Remember that money is simply a means to an end, it is not the end for which you are seeking. Money solves many problems, but wisdom will outsmart money any day. Money is what we use to get the things that we want and need, it does not secure happiness, it does not have a mind of its own. It is a way to secure goods and services nothing more, nothing less. You are the one that controls what you do with your money. Learn to use knowledge to create opportunities to get money, never let money get the best of you.

For self-employed business owners who are experiencing financial stress, one of the best ways to regain financial stability is to put yourself in a position where you know what's going on with your finances at all times. You need a cash budget, this is similar to a standard budget except that a cash budget focuses on the cash items only. Therefore you will include in your budget only your cash collections and cash payments. Your cash collections are all the anticipated direct deposits, electronic transfers coming into your bank account, money orders, cashier's checks and actual cash that you will be receiving for the month. Your collections could be interest, dividends, profits from business equity, rent income, savings withdrawal, etc. The cash payments are usually all the payments that you are obligated to pay for that month. If you realize that you may be coming up short on cash, use the cash management strategies discussed in chapter eight. The reason a cash budget is recommended in this situation is because it is a more conservative approach to cash management. It reduces the possibility of disappointments from bounced checks, or any other debts owed to you. Once the checks have been converted to cash, then you can include it in your cash budget. This form of budgeting will provide you with a more realistic idea of what your finances will look like so that you can plan using more concrete figures. It also offers peace of mind and provides you with assurance.

CONSIDER THIS...

Sometimes solopreneurs experience challenges getting financing because they cannot show steady income, or incurred a loss in their business which may hinder them from even buying a home. Such situations can be very frustrating adding further tension to a financial situation. Hold steady, if you have been denied financing, find out what you need to get what you want. Implement an action plan to obtain what you need, then work towards achieving that goal. The alternative is to find another way to get what you need or want. Do your research and speak with a professional in that particular industry who can offer you some guidance. Sometimes you may have to go back to the basics in order to propel yourself forward.

Cash Budget Example

Cash Collections

Beginning cash balance	$ 5,700
Income from business	$ 2,500
Income from rents	$ 1,500
Spouse monthly salary	$ 3,500
Total Cash Available	$ 13,200

Cash Payments

Mortgage on home	$ (1,500)
Utilities	$ (350)
Phone	$ (90)
Internet	$ (50)
Food	$ (600)
Total amount needed to cover bills	$ (2,590)
Excess Cash	**$ 10,610**

Figure 10.1

Cash Budget Formula

Beginning cash balance (previous month's ending balance)
+ Cash Collections
= **Total Cash available to pay bills**
- Cash Payments
= **Excess Cash or Cash shortage amount**

Figure 10.2

A Cash Budget is an excellent tool for managing both personal and business funds. If you want to maintain a minimum cash balance in your bank account at all times, exclude that amount from the available cash for use.

BE IN CONTROL NOT CONTROLLED

Sometimes while on a road trip with family or friends they may begin to offer advice and tell you how to drive, little things like signal before you turn, watch out for the car ahead of you, questioning if you know where you are going, suggesting where you should park the car and even telling you when to stop and fill up on gas. Jokingly, these people are referred to as back-seat-drivers. People whom you never sought their advice, but they continue to offer you unsolicited directional guidance and their opinions on how you are driving. They can actually become very annoying and even cause an accident if you do not maintain control of your focus as the driver. Be very careful when around these type of personalities. Some of them care about your success and really want to see you do well, but they don't realize how tiring it is to constantly hear their complaints or unsolicited advice. While others are downright sarcastic, jealous and think very little of you, they are even shocked that you have been able to build a business. Do not let them control you, do not let their words intimidate you, do not entertain them, do not invite them into your space. Keep the negative energy away from your place of business; do not even tell them what is happening in your businesses. That old myth about "sticks and stones may break my bones, but words will never hurt me" is a lie!

Words have a way of penetrating deep into a person's mind and making its home there, and negative thoughts can have a damaging effect on people. If you struggle with negative thinking, make an effort to change your thoughts by deliberately thinking on more positive things and stay away from people who don't encourage you. Sometimes people comment on what they do not understand or based on what they perceive, but you should know and appreciate the people who care genuinely about your success. Welcome the honest feedback about things in your life worth rethinking from those who truly care about you, but think over the recommendations carefully before taking action. Be diplomatic in your response and try to keep yourself from getting upset. Think of your customers, prospects, and the image of your business before you act. Apply the same principles to your social media sites. At times, it is not family or friends, but business acquaintances who think highly of themselves and may treat you as if you are insignificant. Take nothing to heart and stay focused on your business, it's all about reaching your goals and these people are just distractions. Remember, you are responsible for your business, if you get off focus it's your life and that of your family that will be impacted, not theirs. Further, it is your money that will lose the potential returns, not theirs. Most people that you come in contact with will not be in your business circles in a few years, because people move on to other opportunities, they may relocate to a different city or even find other associations to join, and you can choose to do the same.

If you lack confidence, get the help you need to regain confidence and maintain your focus. Continue to expand your knowledge by learning, hang around people who will encourage you, meditate and pray for wisdom and strength, only seek advice from those who you admire and respect. If you don't know anyone personally who you admire, then the read books, listen to audios or watch the videos of the experts who you respect and can learn from. Many people have journeyed through the path that you are on and have left advice worth reading or listening to. However, for the people who truly care about you, if they persist in offering you unsolicited advice, lovingly let them know that you appreciate their care and concern, but you have got things under control, and if you need their advice you will let them know.

LET YOUR DESTINATION BE YOUR MOTIVATION

Sometimes the hardest thing to do is staying motivated, to run your race without becoming weary, to keep your eyes on the road ahead so that you can realize your dreams. Many of the things that people do started because of a dream that they had inside them, or an idea they thought was good. The possibilities of what can be realized from carrying out their ideas is what motivated them into action. With that in mind, we can say that motivation comes from within you, not necessarily from another person. All too often people rely on the approval of others, as if these people hold the keys to their destiny. They rarely listen to what their instinct is telling them, and after many years they realize that they have been living someone else's dream instead of their own. Obtaining guidance from someone with more experience is a part of life and recommended. But, the purpose of guidance is to help you see things from another perspective; perhaps insights that you may not have conceived because it can only be obtained through experience.

Guidance is not a directive, an order that must be followed. Guidance is counsel and you should weigh the recommendation and opinions of others wisely. The insights and perspectives should be considered carefully so that you can make the best possible decision. People usually share advice based on what they have learned through their experiences in life, in their career, or from what others have shared with them. If someone is offering you guidance in an area that they have never experienced, you may want to leave the advice on the table. Sometimes there are situations where no one can help you, in these moments pray for guidance, trust your instincts and make the best possible decision. Most successful people stepped out by faith hoping that the ideas they have put into action will begin to take shape and evolve. Running a business is not a walk in the park, it requires tenacity. So, let your desire to arrive at your destination motivate you each day to go the extra mile, and let your hope of the life you seek be your inspiration. Keep your vision before you and let your determination to create a better life for you and your family move you to be disciplined enough to do the work needed to achieve your goals. Never be afraid to put forth your ideas, take calculated risk (*Mindful of the worst case scenario, but moving forward with a plan*), and never stop believing. Be prepared to walk your journey alone if you must, view these times as opportunities to focus on the task at hand. It's like being on an expressway when the roads are clear, you can speed up and get to your destination much faster. Be optimistic and diligent with your work, because you get out of your business what you put into it.

NOTES

1. "Geographic Area Series: Nonemployer Statistics by Receipt Size Class: 2012 more information 2012 Nonemployer Statistics", United States Census Bureau American Fact Finder 2014. http://factfinder2.census.gov.

2. Kiyosaki, Robert T. "Why "A" Students Work for "C" Students: Plata Publishing, LLC, 2013.

3. Spiceland, David, Thomas, Wayne, and Herrmann, Don. Financial Accounting-Second Edition: McGraw Hill, 2011.

4. Spilker, Brian, Ayers, Ben, Robinson, John, Outslay, Ed, Worsham, Ron, Barrick, John, Weaver, Connie. Taxation of Individuals and Business Entities-2014 Edition: McGraw Hill/Irwin.

5. The U.S. Small Business Administration: Personal Financial Statements, http://www.sba.gov/content/personal-financial-statement.

6. United States Internal Revenue Service: Publication 15, 2014.

7. United States Internal Revenue Service: Employment Taxes, http://www.irs.gov/Businesses/Small- Businesses-&-Self-Employed/Employment-Taxes-2.

8. United States Internal Revenue Service: Form 1040-ES Estimated Tax for Individuals, 2014.

INDEX